WHERE DOES FREEDOM END AND TYRANNY BEGIN?

How did we get here and where are we headed?

GLORIA COLLI COUNSELLOR

NEWMAN SPRINGS PUBLISHING
320 Broad Street
Red Bank, NJ 07701

First originally published by Newman Springs Publishing 2021

ISBN 978-1-63692-305-5 (Paperback)
ISBN 978-1-63692-306-2 (Hardcover)
ISBN 978-1-63692-307-9 (Digital)

Printed in the United States of America

This book is dedicated to all the brave men and women of our armed forces, police and law enforcement officers, federal agents, and fire-fighters—past, present, and future.

For those past warriors, may you forever rest in peace. You have my gratitude for the ultimate sacrifice you made for our nation, our safety, and our freedom.

For our present warriors, may God bless you, give you strength, and bring you home safely to your loved ones and your grateful country.

Thank you for your service and for keeping us the land of the free and the home of the brave! God bless you, and God bless America!

CONTENTS

ACKNOWLEDGMENTS

My love and gratitude go out to my children, Dawn and Jay, my grandchildren, and my loving family and friends for their encouragement and support. I love you all!

I am also grateful for the inspiration of our religious leaders, especially my pastor, Reverend Monsignor Edward J. Kurtyka, and our music director, Ryan Petrie. They have been helping all of us in St. Paul's Parish get through this difficult time by keeping us together in prayer with the livestreamed masses and opening our church once again.

Thank you too to my new friends in Christ—William Whited and his wife, Patty—for sharing their story with me and allowing me to share it with you.

My heartfelt thanks to Taylor Wolf for aiding me with your computer and social media skills!

INTRODUCTION: THE POWER OF EXPRESSION

No one can dispute the fact that we, human beings, have an innate need to express our feelings. I believe we can all agree that when we have something on our minds, we would have a hard time holding back. That is certainly true for me. We especially want to share our feelings with those closest to us because they are the ones we feel safest with. Unfortunately for them, they often get the brunt of our feelings and emotions—good and bad.

Expressing our feelings is important to our physical and emotional health. There are consequences to keeping everything inside. It stands to reason that holding in pent-up feelings can lead to stress, anxiety, disappointment, and depression. You don't have to take my word for it. Just take a look at the many commercials on television and in magazines for pills that are touted to help fight depression, anxiety, insomnia, and digestive issues.

There are a wide range of feelings we experience throughout the course of our lives, which include but are not limited to love, hate, joy, sorrow, happiness, sadness, peace, anxiety, disappointment, and, the worst one of all, fear. Fear, I believe, is in a class by itself. It causes us to make poor judgments, form wrong conclusions, and, in some cases, lead to bad decisions that can alter the course of our life.

Feelings are composed of good energy and bad energy. Sadly, some of us sometimes expend more energy hiding our feelings than expressing them, which can lead to unnecessary problems. When all is said and done, our feelings—and how we express them—are personal; they are an intimate part of who we are. They define us.

We express ourselves in many ways—for example, laughter, tears, music, writing, arts, sports, prayer, meditation, or possibly a long talk with a best friend or just spending some quiet time with a significant other or spouse. One may even break a dish or two. No kidding! I recently saw an advertisement for a company that rents out space to customers who want to let off steam by breaking things. Customers can bring their own breakables with them or, for an added cost, they can buy them from the store. They say that these activities relieve stress, anxiety, anger, and other bad-energy emotions.

For me, I always try to look to high-energy endeavors, such as meditation, prayer, exercise, yoga, or a long walk—any of which I find almost immediately calming and peaceful. Reading or answering a good crossword puzzle helps me get to sleep faster.

I think many of us can attest to the fact that when we feel content and at peace, we also feel more powerful. If we pay attention, we see that those are the times we are most successful. Everything seems to fall into place. I do not believe it is luck or coincidence. Spiritual awareness not only enlightens us but also brings out the power within each of us.

There are benefits to sharing our feelings with others. For example, sharing allows us to become more connected to the people around us, especially those who mean the most to us. When we honestly express our thoughts and feelings with others, it is an indication of our affection for them and, more importantly, our trust in them. Likewise, when others share their feelings with us, they are demonstrating their trust in us. So the question becomes "What holds some people back?" What would make us keep our thoughts and feelings in? Fear of rejection? Insecurity?

When we are feeling confident and in control, we are more likely to speak up and share our thoughts and feelings. If we are feeling vulnerable, insecure, or unsure of ourselves, we are more likely to remain silent for fear of criticism or, worse, rejection. It is human nature to want to be liked and accepted.

I know if someone asks me my opinion, whether it be a trivial matter or something of great importance, I will give an honest and complete answer. If you asked my children though, they may say *too* complete. I admit I have been known to get too "wordy" sometimes. I am truthful to a fault, but sometimes that is a slippery slope. I always do my best to avoid hurting anyone's feelings as, I believe, we all should.

In today's social climate, we may be eager to speak our minds or share our views or opinions, but we do not for fear of the backlash that often comes, sad to say. I remember the time when a healthy debate of opposing views was not only possible but welcomed. Listening to both sides of an issue, at best, increased our knowledge and, at the least, gave us something to think about. Being on the other side of an issue didn't make enemies out of friends or relatives. Unfortunately, that is not the case today. I have even heard of divorces occurring because of political differences!

Some issues, especially politics and religion, can lead to a toxic environment today. We must be careful at work, in school, or even during family gatherings. It is a frightening time. A time to reflect on our rights as Americans to free speech, a free press, to worship, and to own and bear arms.

There are so many contrary views and misinformation on social media and pundits in mainstream media that I felt compelled to read these important amendments to our Constitution and confirm the facts for myself. I have been encouraging my family and those within my sphere of influence to do the same. No sense debating, I tell them, "Read it for yourself."

But I digress. Earlier, I was talking about how we express our feelings, which is how I got the idea to write in the first place. The more I thought about it, the more committed I became to putting pen to paper to express my views on the scary and unprecedented times we are living through in America today. These are my views as an American, my views as a United States Navy veteran and patriot, my views as a senior citizen, my views as a mom and grandmother, and my views as a Christian.

I believe our beloved country is headed for a "perfect storm." Only we, American citizens, can right our course.

THE STATE OF OUR UNION

When I began writing this book, it started out as a book of poetry with an introduction on how we humans express ourselves. So you may well ask how my idea for this book took a sudden turn to the right. My answer? Because of the dramatic turn to the left the Socialist Democrat Party has taken.

I was well into the writing when I began to see reports of one egregious event after another on the news and on the Internet. I was stunned by what was happening across our country. America is unrecognizable to me today. First, the COVID-19 pandemic took us over, and as if that isn't difficult enough to deal with, we are now witnessing our country being torn apart by anarchists.

Antifa and Black Lives Matter, a Marxist organization, and other anti-American groups are highjacking peaceful protests and leading the riots, looting, and destruction of many of our great cities. And to what purpose? There is one obvious answer—anarchy. Or could it be something even more sinister? Dire consequences are looming here.

We are bombarded with words like "woke," which is a political term of African American origin. It refers to a perceived awareness of issues concerning social justice and racial justice. It is derived "from the African-American Vernacular English expression 'stay woke,' whose grammatical aspect refers to a continuing awareness of these issues" (*Wikipedia*).

"Cancel culture" is another term frequently used which refers to the popular practice of withdrawing support for (or canceling) public figures and companies after they have done or said something considered to be objectionable or offensive. It is generally discussed as being performed on social media in the form of group shaming (Dictionary.com).

In the article "Welcome to America's Cultural Revolution," it states that "only approved thought is permitted." *National Review's* David Harsanyi further wrote on June 9, 2020: "We're in the dawn of a high-tech, bloodless Cultural Revolution; one that relies on intimidation, public shaming, and economic ruin to dictate what words and ideas are permissible in the public square." More on this to follow.

The more I learned, the more concerned I became. So I felt compelled to change course and write about life and events occurring in our country today, the course of events that got us here, and what we can likely expect in the future. No, I do not have a crystal ball, but what I do know is that our country is at a crossroads. From my point of view, I see two paths for our country. Two paths that would take our country in two totally different directions, depending on which path we choose.

The Socialist Democrat Party would take us to increased erosion of our liberties and a radical Socialist agenda of raising taxes, padding the Supreme Court, ending our energy independence by limiting and/or eliminating fracking, giving China a pass, and threatening our trade agreements. As Maya Angelou once said, "When someone shows you who they are, believe them the first time." As a patriotic American, to say that I am concerned is an understatement.

We are living through tumultuous and frightening times today. We are still in the throes of the COVID-19 coronavirus global pandemic which, according to the evidence brought forth to date, indicates it originated in the virology lab in Wuhan, China, and was allowed to spread from China to the rest of the world.

Our country is under attack on many fronts, and as in the past, the American people will provide the defense by standing up for America and our freedom by making our voices heard. "In history, nothing happens by accident. If it happened, you can bet someone planned it" (Franklin Delano Roosevelt, thirty-second US president).

What started out as peaceful protests following the George Floyd murder in Minneapolis, Minnesota, by a police officer while in custody turned into chaos, lawlessness, and mayhem. The peaceful protesters' message has been all but drowned out in the midst of the riots.

Our country, our Constitution, and our very way of life is being threatened by Antifa, Black Lives Matter, radical Socialist Democrats, anarchists, anti-American protesters, rioters, and the big-money Globalists that are financing them.

Rioters are bringing down historic statues, burning our great American flag—a symbol of our freedom and liberty—and taking over parts of our large cities and communities. Their goal is to erase our history and remake our country.

Former vice president Joe Biden, the Democrat nominee for president, said he is on board. He has said that if elected, "he would transform our country." Transform it into what exactly?

Many riots and protests are happening simultaneously. For example, there was a movement whose goal is to destroy Mount Rushmore, in South Dakota, coincidentally coinciding with President Trump's visit to the monument. Mount Rushmore is a national memorial honoring four great presidents. It represents the history of our great country and their legacies—the history the cancel culture is trying so hard to erase.

On Tuesday, June 30, 2020, Congress debated whether "In God We Trust" should be the national motto. Of course, it already is the national motto, guaranteed by an act of Congress in 1956, and "In God We Trust" had already been reaffirmed once before as the national motto, by another act of Congress in 2002.

"Is God? Or is man God? In God do we trust, or in man do we trust?" asked Representative Trent Franks (representative from Arizona). He was laying out the deeper meaning behind this debate, saying, "It was a chance for the House to reassert that it believes there is divine goodness and order in the universe." If there isn't, Franks said, "We should just let anarchy prevail because, after all, we are just worm food. So indeed we have the time to reaffirm that God is God and in God we do trust."

Thank God for the courage of Congressman Trent Franks and his voice of reason. Unfortunately, all the subversive behavior we are witnessing is being ignored, condoned, or even celebrated by the mainstream media, social media, and the radical Socialist Democrats. Ironically, most—if not all—of the cities affected by the rioting, looting, and destruction are led by Democrat mayors and governors. Never in my wildest dreams did it ever occur to me that I would live to see the likes of which going on in America today.

Antifa and Black Lives Matter activists are taking over neighborhoods and business districts with armed thugs who are holding neighborhoods hostage as they threaten to keep out the police and destroy business communities. They are burning down and looting businesses, firebombing police cars, and destroying neighborhoods. And to what purpose?

So let's examine the facts about the Black Lives Matter organization. The Black Lives Matter website reads:

> #BlackLivesMatter was founded in 2013 in response to the acquittal of Trayvon Martin's murderer. Black Lives Matter Foundation, Inc. is a global organization in the US, UK, and Canada, whose mission is to eradicate white supremacy and build local power to intervene in violence inflicted on Black communities by the state and vigilantes. By combating and countering acts of violence, creating space for Black imagination and innovation, and centering Black joy, we are winning immediate improvements in our lives.
>
> We are expansive. We are a collective of liberators who believe in inclusive and spacious movement. We also believe that in order to win and bring as many people with us along the way, we must move beyond the narrow nationalism that is all too prevalent in Black communities. We must ensure we are building a movement that brings all of us to the front.
>
> We affirm the lives of Black queer and trans folks, disabled folks, undocumented folks, folks

with records, women, and all Black lives along the gender spectrum.

According to a June 23, 2020, post by Brandon Morse: "You're being duped: Black Lives Matter founder admits 'We are Trained Marxists'" in resurfaced video. See it on YouTube. It is obvious that this is a Marxist group hiding behind a slogan.

Since New Year's Day in 2010, there have been more than twelve thousand shootings in Chicago. More than fourteen thousand people were injured in those shootings, including more than two thousand who have died, many of them young children, according to Midway, Chicago Lawn, and Ashburn. Sadly, those numbers are growing each day.

Our youth is our treasure, but the Black Lives Matter organization is not protesting or condemning the deaths of these children in Chicago, Atlanta, and other parts of the country. Why? Don't these Black lives matter?

On June 27, 2020, *The Atlantic* printed an article written by Tom McTague on June 24, 2020, titled "The Decline of the American World." He wrote, "Other countries are used to loathing America, admiring America, and fearing America (sometimes all at once). But pitying America? That one is new."

What is happening in America today is not only shameful; it is dangerous. We have to ask ourselves, "How did this happen? Where did this start?"

The murder of George Floyd by a police officer while Floyd was in custody began the protests, but peaceful protests were soon hijacked and turned into riots, looting, and the destruction of private and public property. So why did radical Socialist Democrat mayors and governors get on board with the destruction of their cities? One reason that stands out to me is the presidential election of November 3, 2020 (by the time this book is published, it would have already taken place).

I believe the radical Socialist Democrat Party and their supporters would do and have done anything to thwart President Trump's agenda or prevent his reelection. Evidence of this can be seen in what has come to light since the Mueller report, the impeachment of our president over a benign phone call to Ukraine, the spying on the Trump candidacy and presidency in 2016, and the suspect handling of the General Michael Flynn matter by the FBI. Evidence has come to light that has led to the dropping of those charges against General Flynn by the Justice Department. "FBI notes that show that FBI misconduct led to the criminal charge against General Flynn," according to *The Detroit News*.

In fact, according to Courthousenews.com, FBI lawyer Kevin Clinesmith was an assistant general counsel for the FBI assigned to support the bureau's Crossfire Hurricane investigation of Russian meddling in the 2016 election and the Trump campaign's suspected facilitation of those efforts.

Clinesmith has been indicted for falsifying records. The indictment notes that the FBI executed a wiretap against individual number 1 under the Foreign Intelligence Surveillance Act (FISA) in October 2016 and that three subsequent applications to approve that warrant were approved over the next year.

> The FBI cited probable cause that the target "was a knowing agent of a foreign power, specifically Russia," but Clinesmith's indictment says the FBI was already informed in August 2016 this individual served as an "operational contact" for an unspecified government agency from 2008 to 2013, and that he had provided the agency with information about his "prior contacts with certain Russian intelligence officers" to that end.

Robert Mueller had been appointed as special counsel to oversee the investigation by May 2017 when the FBI needed to renew the FISA surveillance warrant of Cater Page for the third time.

> It was around this time, however, that Page has asserted publicly that he was a CIA source.

Prosecutors say Clinesmith verified Page's status with a CIA liaison on June 15, 2017, but misrepresented what the liaison told him to incorrectly say that Page was "not a source."…

Clinesmith resigned from the FBI last year and is expected to plead guilty to one count of making a false statement.

This means the Mueller investigation should never have taken place. US Attorney John Durham is expected to complete his investigation this fall, hopefully before the election. Sadly, it doesn't look like that will happen. I hope I am wrong. It appears that the FBI is still withholding important information. A computer repair shop owner gave the FBI a laptop computer allegedly brought to them early this year for repair by Hunter Biden. The owner claims that the computer was never picked up and the owner takes ownership if the computer is not picked up in a stated amount of time. After reading some of the e-mails and viewing some of the pictures, he brought it to the FBI. Thankfully, and unbeknownst to anyone, he kept a copy of the hard drive—a problem for the Bidens and for the FBI, I would think. It seems that the FBI sat on this during the impeachment hearings. If this was known then, the impeachment would not have taken place. The e-mail chain alleges Joe Biden's knowledge of his son's dubious business dealings and possible corruption. Pressure is being put on the FBI, who now claims to be investigating these allegations and the veracity of the laptop and the e-mails.

On September 16, 2020, Senate Homeland Security Committee authorizes subpoenas for testimony from Obama officials—former CIA director John Brennan, former director of National Intelligence Agency James Clapper, former FBI director James Comey, and other Obama administration officials—as part of its broad review into the origins of the Russia investigation.

It looks like the truth about the three-plus years' war on the Trump administration is finally coming to light. But will anyone be held accountable beside Clinesmith?

Director of National Intelligence Radcliffe has recently unclassified more documents that now show that Hillary Clinton authorized, approved, and paid for the debunked Fusion GPS dossier smearing then candidate and later president Donald J. Trump. This dossier was used by then FBI director James Comey to spy on the campaign and his signing of the FISA warrants used to investigate the president for almost all his first term only to find out there was never Russian collusion on the part of the Trump campaign. Rather, it is now proved that the Russian collusion was conducted by Hillary Clinton and the Democratic National Committee. Shameful.

The common consensus of objective citizens is that President Trump is so hated by the Left and their supporters, including the media, because he is the only one standing in the way of the Socialist Democrat agenda of raising taxes, reinstituting restrictive regulations affecting the business community, defunding and transforming law enforcement, and threatening our energy independence and all the progress our economy has made under President Trump's leadership and, maybe most importantly, China. It comes down to this: Capitalism versus Socialism and freedom versus tyranny.

I am praying as I am writing this that God will place his hand on our country and people. Whatever happens, I have great faith in the American way, the American dream, and the love the majority of Americans have for our country. We may have been complacent, but it is not too late to wake up and save our country. It is time for *us* to be woke! The good news is that we have some important things going for us, namely our Constitution, Declaration of Independence, and Bill of Rights as well as the Supreme Court whose job is to uphold and protect them.

Our republic has three branches of government—the executive branch, the legislative branch, and the judicial branch. Each of these branches of government have been designed to protect us from tyranny and overreaching government.

There are currently two movements in this country today—the populist movement to protect the American way of life as we know it and the Socialist movement that is working to transform our country and take away our freedoms albeit a little at a time. It is happening now.

In the past, when our rights were threatened, Americans rose to the occasion. When it matters most, we stand together. Today is no exception, and it has never mattered more. We have a lot to be thankful for and a lot to protect. Yes, things have certainly changed, but we Americans are still the architects of our destiny. We have to start by supporting the restoration of law and order. The facts are now staring us in the face. The reality is now exposed; Democrats have failed the people, and they are complicit in the destruction of the cities they run. This is not like the riots of the past; this is anarchy.

So how does our country today compare to past decades? How did we not see this coming? Or did we?

I felt compelled to explore this because we are on the brink of a cultural revolution that will change the United States of America for decades, if not forever. There are a lot of things at stake for Americans today. We the people are the only ones who can direct the course of our country, but we must have the courage to do so. Our greatest weapon is our voice and our vote. Failure is not an option. If we are to preserve our freedom and way of life as we know it, we Americans must be united. We must be strong. We must be determined, and we must be heard in one united voice.

"Freedom is one of the deepest and noblest aspirations of the human spirit" (President Ronald Reagan).

SO WHERE IS OUR VOICE?

Everywhere man blames nature and fate, yet
his fate is mostly but the echo of his character
and his passions, his mistakes and his weaknesses.
—Democritus

The election of November 3, 2020, will go down in history as the most important election of our time. Make no mistake, it will be a turning point for America. It is critical for faith-based and free-dom-loving Americans, who love our republic and our democracy, to be heard on November 3. If we want to maintain our quality of life and all the freedoms we Americans enjoy under our Constitution, Declaration of Independence, and Bill of Rights, then we must speak out in one loud and united voice. We cannot afford to be complacent or silent any longer.

Whether a Democrat, Republican, or an independent voter, I have to believe that all Americans love our country and our free-dom. What American would want to live under a controlling and Totalitarian regime, one that prefers Socialism over Capitalism? The people who believe the promises of the Left are kidding themselves. If they are taken in, then they too will someday suffer. United we stand; divided we fall.

The only ones that will be exempt from their tyranny is the power-hungry, self-serving radical Socialist Democrat political lead-ers themselves. Think about it, they want to take away our Second Amendment right so we cannot defend ourselves, but they have armed guards to protect them. They want to tax the middle class and make us poor and dependent on the government while they grow wealthier, and they want to control our health care while they have the best for themselves. Worse than that, they will have the power over population control—a very scary possibility. Ironically, COVID-19 gives us a glimpse of what that would look like.

Remember, nothing is free. Someone always pays, and it is usually the middle class. By the way, Congress long ago made themselves exempt from the laws and dicta they have imposed on American citizens. Therefore, it is not surprising that they refuse to put term limits on the ballots.

I have often wondered why we the people don't write it in the ballots ourselves. After all, we are the voters, the electorate, are we not? Why don't we have the courage to speak up?

Democrat Speaker of the House Nancy Pelosi has served in Congress, representing San Francisco for thirty-one years. Take a good look at San Francisco today. Once a beautiful American city and tourist attraction, it has deteriorated and appears to be in a downward spiral. The poor Democrat leadership has led to the most homelessness and crime it has ever seen. It is undeniable, a change is long overdue. San Francisco desperately needs new leadership and new ideas that represent the present rather than the past.

It seems that America is on the brink of a cultural revolution. According to *National Review* (June 24, 2020):

> We're in the dawn of a high-tech, bloodless Cultural Revolution; one that relies on intimidation, public shaming, and economic ruin to dictate what words and ideas are permissible in the public square.
>
> "Words are violence" has always been an illiberal notion meant to stifle speech and open discourse. Popularized by a generation of coddled and brittle college students, it now guides policy and editorial pages at [some newspapers] and most major news outlets.

I disagree. This has not been just a "high-tech, bloodless Cultural Revolution." Many people have died. In Chicago alone, sixty-four people were shot, including three innocent children, one only a one-year-old baby. These shootings in Chicago happened in one weekend alone! In broad daylight on a weekday in July 2020, fourteen people were shot and injured while attending a funeral in Chicago!

The mayor of Chicago is refusing the help offered by the president. She has failed her city and yet is refusing help to stem this tide of violence. She claims federal agents have no right to be there and are not welcome in her city. Yet she holds back the police and law enforcement officers that want desperately to do their jobs. But wait a minute, when her home was threatened by the protesters, she ordered the Chicago police to protect her home! When asked about this, Mayor Lightfoot replied that it was important that she be protected because she is the mayor. Wait, what about the people of her city that she was elected to protect? Disgraceful!

How many people, young children among them, must die before something is done to stem the violence? When will the police be allowed to do their job?

At the time of this writing, the federal courthouse and other federal buildings in Portland, Oregon, are under attack. Armed thugs and rioters have been trying to burn the courthouse down for sixty-two days and counting. Many agents protecting the building have been seriously injured, with three of them made blind by lasers deliberately shot at their eyes. This cannot and must not continue. This is America, after all!

Attorney General Barr said he is determined to protect these agents and federal buildings, but the mayor and governor are the only ones that can activate their police to do their jobs and restore peace in their city.

After over two months of violence and destruction and threatened action by the federal government, Governor Brown has finally ordered police to restore the peace and clear out the rioters. However, that did not last.

Today, it was reported that July was the deadliest month in three decades in Portland. On Friday, July 31, 150 rounds were fired outside one apartment building. Bullets flying over his head, one man had to crawl on his hands and knees out of his apartment. He said he felt as though he were in a war zone.

In other major cities in the United States, mayors and governors still insist that they too don't want federal agents in their cities. They claim it is unconstitutional. However, the law is clear.

According to the Bureau of Alcohol, Tobacco, Firearms and Explosives, their responsibilities and their mission is to protect communities from violent criminals, criminal organizations, the illegal use and trafficking of firearms, the illegal use and storage of explosives, acts of arson and bombings, acts of terrorism, and the illegal diversion of alcohol and tobacco products.

Justice Manual title 9-66.010 reads in part: "One of the principal responsibilities of the federal criminal law is the protection of government property. The property holdings of the United States, its departments and agencies are extensive and include both real and personal property in this country and abroad."

40 US Code 1315 states, "Pursuant to the Homeland Security Act of 2002, the Secretary of Homeland Security shall protect the buildings, grounds, and property that are owned, occupied, or secured by the Federal Government (including any agency, instrumentally, or wholly owned or mixed-ownership corporation thereof) and the persons on the property."

In Seattle, Washington, two African American teenagers were shot and killed—Horace Lorenzo Anderson, a nineteen-year-old, and a sixteen-year-old. Another fourteen-year-old African American youth and an adult are in intensive care at the time of this writing.

In all, there were four shootings, one reported rape, and over sixty-five robberies, assaults, and injuries to date.

Los Angeles has seen an unprecedented growth in homicides, as has New York City; Baltimore, Maryland; Chicago, Illinois; Minneapolis, Minnesota; Madison and Milwaukee, Wisconsin; Kansas City, Missouri; Albuquerque, New Mexico; Atlanta, Georgia; and the list goes on. All these cities are run by Democrat mayors and governors who have tied the hands of their police with stand-down orders that allow crime to run rampant. So where is the voice of their citizens, or why are they being ignored? Hopefully, their voices will be heard in November.

Operation Legend launched by Attorney General Barr is named after LeGend Taliferro, the four-year-old boy who was shot while he slept in his own bed in Kansas City, Missouri. According to the Attorney General, "The operation is a sustained, systematic and coordinated law enforcement initiative across all federal law enforcement agencies working in conjunction with state and local law enforcement officials to fight the sudden surge of violent crime, beginning in Kansas City, Missouri." Operation Legend was created as a result of President Trump's promise to assist America's cities that are plagued by recent violence according to the Department of Justice Office of Public Affairs on Wednesday, July 8, 2020.

Some of the largest cities across our nation are being beset by mobs, many armed, burning flags, tearing down historic statues, and defacing monuments. In Washington DC, unarmed National Guard are protecting our monuments, historic statues, and St. John's Episcopal Church, known as "the Presidents' Church," which rioters tried to burn down in early June 2020. This effort against our historic monuments, houses of worship, historic buildings, and statues is an assault on our civilization. It is a total breakdown of law and order. If told this six months ago in January, I would not have believed it possible in the United States of America.

The cities that are experiencing the most destruction are cities and states led by Liberal Democrat mayors and governors, who are sitting back and letting it happen. They are deliberately adding to the problem by ignoring the chaos. They should not need to be reminded that it is the responsibility and sacred duty of our elected officials to protect the people that elected them. It is astonishing that they would let their cities be destroyed for political reasons.

Mayor Wheeler of Portland, Oregon, not only condones the violence in his city; he is actually instigating it. After almost two months of protests and rioting, Mayor Wheeler attempted to talk to protesters in front of the federal courthouse they were trying to burn. He began by saying, "I stand with you." However, he did so amid boos and jeers and calls for him to resign. When federal agents tried to remove the mob from the front of the federal courthouse, they met heavy resistance as bricks and other objects too gross to mention were thrown at them. The mob was tear-gassed, with Mayor Wheeler in the midst of them. Only then was Mayor Wheeler escorted by his five-armed security guards out of the area.

In August 2020, the mob proceeded to the condominium building that Mayor Wheeler lives in. Shortly thereafter, he announced that he was moving out of his condo and putting it up for sale. He did not say where he was moving to.

I have a question, "What about the citizens of Portland, Oregon, who cannot afford to move?" What about their destroyed businesses?

President Trump has repeatedly offered to send help to stem the violence in Portland and other affected cities. "We can take care of this in a half hour, if they asked for our help."

It is incomprehensible to me that political leaders, like Mayor Wheeler, who were elected by their constituents to protect them do just the opposite. Ironically, Mayor Wheeler is being opposed in the election by an Antifa activist. How did that happen? Portland citizens are asked to choose between an unpopular and incompetent mayor and an Antifa activist? By the way, the Justice Department just named Antifa as a terrorist organization. Shouldn't it be against the law for a domestic terrorist to run for elected government office? I'm just saying.

In September, Governor Di Santis of Florida introduced a bill that would make it a crime punishable by six months in jail for anyone harming a citizen or a police officer during a violent uprising or riot. Excuse me, but it was always my understanding that there are laws protecting citizens as well as police officers. These laws protect against assault and battery. We have to ask ourselves, "Why aren't they being enforced now?" The bill would also eliminate funding of any municipality that defunded their police departments. Rioting and looting would be punished with jail time. I say it's about time a governor took some action against this mayhem. I believe it is time for the citizens of these cities and states to take a hard look at the people they have elected.

In light of present circumstances and the deterioration of their communities, they and the citizens of other Democrat cities affected by the violence would be well advised to rethink their choices and change course. Not doing so will mean the utter destruction of their cities, economies, and quality of life. Governors of these states should take a page from Governor Di Santis's playbook and restore law and order by penalizing the perpetrators of this violence and ending this tyranny.

The federal government has now identified three states as being anarchist states. It is, in my opinion, a no-brainer. We must save our country, or we will be in for a fight.

"The main obstacle to a stable and just world order is the United States of America" (George Soros). George Soros—born Gyorgy Schwartz in Budapest, Hungary, on August 12, 1930—is a left-wing billionaire investor and philanthropist. George Soros said in a statement that the COVID-19 pandemic had "laid bare the fault lines and injustices of our world," according to Lisi Niesner of Reuters.

According to the *New York Times*, Soros, the billionaire philanthropist and Liberal financier, is directing more than $130 million through the organization he founded, the Open Society Foundations, and is making two large grants to nonprofits linked to the government of New York City, which is the epicenter of the coronavirus outbreak in the United States with more than ten thousand deaths because of the virus.

The first grant will provide $20 million to create an Immigrant Emergency Relief Program to provide direct, one-time payments to up to twenty thousand immigrant families who are excluded from the federal relief program, including undocumented immigrants.

Americans are worried. We are uncertain about the future and are frightened by what we see, but where is our voice? We must be heard!

THE FOURTH ESTATE

So now let's take a look at the Fourth Estate and the mainstream media in our country.

The Media Research Center chronicled back in 2011 how Globalist, George Soros, has ties to thirty news outlets in the mainstream media. He has donated millions of dollars to the Democrat Party and continues to do so in an attempt to foster Globalism (Socialism) and the election of Democrats.

Remember the newspaper that touted, "All the news that's fit to print"? Or "The news, nothing but the news," from another news outlet? When did those worthy sentiments go out the proverbial window? News outlets and reporting are unrecognizable today from the past. Now we have "spin doctors" on cable news programs that give opinion rather than reporting the straight news. Are true journalists a thing of the past? Are they now just political operatives?

One of the few conservative outlets, Fox News, has been exposing the assault on President Donald Trump and his supporters from the start of his candidacy and throughout his term as president. They have exposed the lies and misleading information fed by Liberal cable news networks and the mainstream media. They were criticized by the Left, but as time goes on, they have been proven correct.

The bottom line is that the mainstream media is the left-wing arm of the radical Socialist Democrat Party.

The charges by corrupt FBI agents against General Michael Flynn, the president's original national security advisor, have been ordered dropped by Attorney General William Barr when exculpatory evidence came to light that had been previously withheld. Flynn and his family went through three years of hell. He lost his house and had to file for bankruptcy. The mainstream media went after General

Flynn with a vengeance. Even when they are proved wrong, there are never apologies; it is just ignored.

It is shameful. The Left is still fighting to keep the charges alive. The Liberal judge that heard the case is still loath to drop the charges and is appealing, if you can believe that! Disgraceful.

It is anticipated that US Attorney John Durham will be concluding his investigation into this and other matters by fall. One indictment has been made so far. Kevin Clinesmith, assistant general counsel to the FBI, has pled guilty to falsifying a document. It is being reported that other indictments will be forthcoming and the responsible parties will finally be held accountable. I pray that is the case, but in this political climate, nothing is certain.

Senator Lyndsay Graham, chairman of the judiciary committee, has subpoenaed former FBI director James Comey, former director of the National Intelligence Agency James Clapper, and former CIA director John Brennan to testify before the committee.

Former FBI director Comey appeared in front of the committee, and it was a frustrating ordeal. Comey's answer to most of the questions was "I don't recall" or "I don't remember that." In essence, he threw his former colleagues under the bus.

Andrew McCabe decided not to testify following Comey's testimony. It seems the wheels of justice are moving more slowly these days.

In the meantime, we are entitled to a fair and just judiciary and a legal system that operates under the premise that no one is above the law and everyone is treated equally. Unfortunately, that has not been the case since President Trump announced his candidacy. Since then, he has been attacked with lies by the Democrats and the mainstream media and with nonstop investigations. Even when the lies are exposed, they continue the onslaught.

Apparently, the deep state and the establishment have a lot to hide. They did not want an outsider in the White House who would do what Donald J. Trump, the candidate, promised. He promised to "drain the swamp," and that is exactly what he has done. He has exposed the corruption, and so their hate grows.

Imagine if Hillary had been elected. We would have been none the wiser, and America would probably have quietly succumbed to the Left. Thank God she didn't, and Donald J. Trump prevailed.

It is remarkable that President Trump was able to accomplish so much in the face of the "fake news," the unjust investigations, lies, and even an impeachment, which, as it turns out, would never have happened if the truth had come out. Ironically, the telephone call with the Ukraine president was in fact a "good call" as President Trump said. He was right to ask about the corruption in the country and how it related to the Biden family. The truth is finally coming out.

The corrupt media isn't anything new, although it is more exposed today. Mark Levin's book, *Unfreedom of the Press*, tells the story in depth and a lot more eloquently than I. He has researched and studied the Fourth Estate for years. Chapter 6 in his book speaks particularly to the *New York Times*. It is an eye-opener.

The corruption and manipulation of the news started decades ago and may even have changed the course of history. Nazi Germany and the Holocaust is one example. According to Levin's book (see chapter 6), the *New York Times* declined to print (or printed very little) about the persecution and mass murder of the Jews as well as Catholics and other ethnic groups Hitler singled out for annihilation in Germany and Europe. Ironically, the owners of the *New York Times* were Jewish. According to Levin's book, when asked why they didn't cover the story, their reply was to the effect that they did not want to be known as only a Jewish newspaper.

I can't help but wonder, had light been shone on these atrocities and the public been made aware, would it have made a difference? How many people, I wonder, could have been saved had the Holocaust been publicized while it was happening? Surely, someone knew. Would public and political pressure have made a difference? We will never know. I recommend the book highly; it is an eye-opener and an education in and of itself. You know what they say, knowledge is power.

Another book I recommend is Sean Hannity's book, *Live Free or Die*. These are courageous, honest journalists that love America and are not afraid to tell the truth. They are worth the read.

Another thing that has baffled me is why so many Jews are still staunch Democrats in the face of all that the Democrat Party stood for and was founded on? For starters, it was the party of slavery and anti-Semitism.

Democrats were never true friends of Israel. In fact, seven previous presidents promised to move our embassy from Tel Aviv to Jerusalem, recognizing Jerusalem once again as the capital of Israel. They never did. That is, until President Trump. He promised during his campaign that if elected, he would accomplish it. When he became president, he had the courage to keep his promise. In my opinion, he set things right.

One of the arguments against it by the Democrats was the cost. They erroneously estimated the cost would be in the millions. President Trump found a property in Jerusalem, bought it, and renovated it for a total cost of approximately $500,000—one of the benefits of having a builder and a businessman in the White House.

People are not speaking up. Good citizens are worried and concerned. But where is their voice? People are frightened and rightly so. These are scary times indeed, but we need to speak up. We must be heard! Even before the protests started, citizens have been reluctant to express their views. Probably because of the divisiveness of politics. Expressing an opposing view is a dangerous proposition today.

In today's social climate, speaking our mind about politics or related issues could start a debate that could cost us our friendships and our jobs and estrange us from relatives or even our own spouses. It is no wonder we are reluctant to share our views. I am speaking from experience. I have lost one of my Liberal friends, and even a few family members refuse to hear an opposing view. As time goes on, however, keeping silent and being passive will prove to be even more dangerous. Keeping our freedom and our rights depend on our standing up for them. So with families being divided, friendships on the verge of being destroyed, and even our relationships in the workplace in jeopardy, how do we get our point across? Will we ever feel free to speak our minds again?

I think it will take time, but I am hopeful that we will regain that freedom. We must. A major priority for all Americans should be to maintain our First Amendment right to free speech, freedom of religion, and peaceful assembly. Remember the saying "You don't know what you have until you lose it"? Once you let a freedom be taken away, you will not be able to get it back!

In my opinion, it is most important today that we always maintain a dialogue with our children. Especially in the arena of education today, it is important to know what our kids are being taught. We must start with making sure our children are educated and not indoctrinated or brainwashed by Liberal Socialist Democrat teachers and professors. I have been stunned to hear young people today deny American history. Indeed, they have been taught to believe more in propaganda than history.

On September 18, 2020, President Trump signed an executive order that schools' curriculums include teaching American history and promoting patriotism again. For example, most young adults under forty do not know about the Holocaust. They are unaware that six million plus Jews were murdered by Nazi Germany. History should be taught accurately—the good, the bad, and the ugly.

Our young nation is still evolving and growing. Immigrants from all over the world try to immigrate to our great country for the freedoms and opportunities America offers.

Some of our young people question some of the greatest achievements of the United States of America, even our moon landing in 1969! I couldn't believe my ears! I decided to refresh my memory by doing some research about our missions to the moon. After doing so, I decided to write about it here, in case other parents and grandparents, like myself, decide to set the young conspiracy theorists straight with a little history lesson.

After our first moon landing on July 20, 1969, the United States had three more missions to the moon—Apollo 15, Apollo 16, and Apollo 17.

On August 17, 1971, astronauts David R. Scott and James B. Irwin completed the first of the three missions on Apollo 15. During the crew's three space walks, Scott and Irwin spent almost nineteen hours exploring the moon's surface and covered seventeen and one-half miles of lunar terrain in the lunar rover. They brought back rocks and lunar dust samples to Earth, but the most significant find was a lunar rock nicknamed the Genesis Rock, sample number 15415. This rock was an anorthosite, a piece of the moon's primordial crust. Although not the oldest brought back, geologists at the Manned Spacecraft Center in Houston, Texas, concluded that this rock was about four billion years old. Apollo 15 was the first of three J missions, often called the true scientific missions to the moon. After the splashdown, the astronauts were trapped in a NASA trailer to be quarantined, in case they brought back any germs or diseases from the moon. They even wore special biological containment suits when they walked out onto the deck of US Navy ship, *The Hornet*, after being retrieved.

On December 14, 1972, Gene Cernan was the last human to walk on the moon. Cernan had this to say from the moon's surface:

> Bob, this is Gene, and I'm on the surface, and as I take man's last steps from the surface [of the moon] for some time to come, but we believe not too long into the future. I'd like to just list what I believe history will record, that America's challenge of today, has forged man's destiny of tomorrow. And, as we leave the Moon at Taurus Littrow, we leave as we come, and, God willing, as we shall return, with peace and hope for all mankind. Godspeed the crew of Apollo 17.

There were many reasons for Americans not stepping foot on the moon since 1972. One reason was funding. The major oil crisis of 1973 was primarily responsible for a shift in the nation's priorities. Funding was limited to NASA's research and scientific missions in the coming years. Such programs included the development of the

Skylab program in 1973 and the Space Shuttle program as well as a number of robotic probes and satellites.

Many high school and college students show a stunning lack of knowledge of American history. I encourage them to study our great history. They should know that our achievements not only benefit us but the world.

By the way, I hope young people are encouraged to read history. I know I will give this book to the young people in my family. Judging by the questions I hear, I am determined to give them a history lesson. I encourage them to research the facts so that they are knowledgeable when they are faced with propaganda.

I remember how naive and unaware I was as a teenager, but at least I knew history. I was taught love of country and the meaning of patriotism. I was taught love of God and family. Some of the kids today are at a disadvantage because they don't seem to know or, worse, don't seem to care. Or maybe they are just too attached to their cell phones. I not only blame the teachers. I have to wonder, where are their parents on these issues? I see more grandparents teaching their grandchildren today. Seriously, they are as astonished as I am! These young people are our future! Some parents I know are steadfast in their commitment to teach their children the truth by communicating with them and then having them do the research, but sadly, others are not. Most children have their heads down, staring at their cell phones and texting the hours away when they should be reading and learning. I can tell you that as I am talking to some of my grandchildren, they are googling what I am telling them to see if I am correct! Seriously? I wish I started to speak up years ago, but who knew? Better late than never, I always say.

There are other issues besides what and how our children are taught. Many of our students' Liberal teachers and professors stifle their students' right to free speech when the students' views disagree with the Liberal views and opinions they teach.

One such university that comes to mind is Berkeley College in California. Since President Trump's election, they have become exposed, as more and more students and even some teachers are speaking up. I have seen more than one professor or teacher interviewed on television. They tell their story of being shunned by Liberal faculty and then fired from their jobs for not conforming. Does this sound like America to you? Berkeley has routinely prevented conservative guest speakers on its campus. That is, until President Trump threatened to withhold funding to any college or university that infringes on their students' First Amendment right to freedom of speech. This attack on freedom of speech has gone on for years unaddressed. Until now. This is so dangerous!

The schools and universities that hire Liberal teachers and professors that infringe on the rights of their students should be held accountable. Parents that pay the tuitions should also speak up and, if necessary, take their children out of these schools. Our children are entitled to their own thoughts, ideas, and their *freedom of speech*!

Part of a good education is learning about American and world history. This is so important. We need to learn from our past—the good, the bad, and the ugly. We could celebrate the good and learn from mistakes so as not to repeat them.

I believe that there will come a day when this younger generation will look. They may not appreciate it now, but it will be glaringly evident in the future. Either they will give a sigh of relief that they were saved from losing everything worth holding dear or, God forbid, they will lament their foolish choices. I hope it is the former and not the latter. It is not too late yet. Talk about waiting until the last minute!

I don't think it is an exaggeration to say that this election may just be a "do or die" moment in the history of our country. The campaign is on, and it is intense. The mainstream news media's bias is unmistakable. I have never seen anything like it in my lifetime. The CEOs of Twitter and Facebook came before the Senate yesterday to answer to their biased censoring of news that is unfavorable to Joe Biden. Americans want to be free, not censored. Now is the time to be heard. Now is the time to speak up.

WHERE DOES FREEDOM END AND TYRANNY BEGIN?

> I pledge allegiance to the Flag of the United
> States of America, and to the Republic for which
> it stands, one Nation under God, indivisible,
> with liberty and justice for all.
> —Pledge of Allegiance

As Americans we are at a crossroads. It is time to save our country and keep us "indivisible."

First Amendment (Amendment I): "Congress shall make no law respecting an establishment of religion, or prohibiting the free exercise thereof; or abridging the freedom of speech, or of the press; or the right of the people peaceably to assemble, and to petition the Government for a redress of grievances."

Second Amendment (Amendment II) guarantees our right to bear arms: "A well-regulated militia, being necessary to the security of a free state, and the right of the people to bear arms shall not be infringed."

As unbelievable as this sounds, our right to worship and the freedom of religion is being threatened today as never before. The Socialist Democrat goal is a godless society. This cannot be over-stated. We must fight back.

During the week of the Democratic National Convention, the words "under God" were omitted twice in two recitations of the Pledge of Allegiance. I was also dismayed by the fact that our great American flag was nowhere to be seen on that stage. Conversely, the Republican National Convention showed a stage full of our American flags. Patriotic songs, prayers by clergy of all faiths, and testimonials from folks like Alice Johnson, whose life sentence for a nonviolent crime was commuted and later pardoned by President Trump, were highlighted, not Hollywood elites. What a contrast!

Today, rioters are burning down churches and desecrating sacred statues. What is alarming is that they are brazen in these acts, knowing that apparently they are not being stopped or punished. The videos on the news in Philadelphia last night showed looters breaking into stores and stealing whatever they could carry. One man was shown with a lift truck carrying a new washing machine down the street. What appalled me more was that fact that no one stopped him. When asked by a reporter, a police officer at the scene said they were understaffed. I think they are afraid of the confrontation erupting into more violence. I can't blame them, I guess.

Liberal leaders are restricting the police and letting them get away with it. It seems they believe that the destruction and chaos is worth it if President Trump is not reelected. They need to be reminded that they were elected to protect their citizens and communities and not to let businesses and communities burn and be destroyed and not let crime to rule. Are these the kind of leaders we want to govern us?

We don't hear about statues being torn down so much anymore since President Trump signed an order to enforce a law that calls for a ten-year mandatory jail sentence for anyone convicted of taking down public historic statues. Incredible as it sounds, that was all it took to stop the takedown of statues.

The burning down of our cities and the rioting and looting is another matter. They say that the rioting and violence will continue whoever wins the presidential election. Sad to say, the looters are those that are using any excuse to steal.

The Left's evil goal is to eventually erase God from our society. If people don't believe in God, a Totalitarian government can have control of the governed through their total dependence on the government. Too many men and women have died to protect our cherished freedoms. The First Amendment guaranteeing our right to free speech, peaceful assembly, and religious freedom are under attack. The Second Amendment and our right to bear arms is also in jeopardy.

My own grandparents immigrated to the United States from Italy. My father's parents came here from Sicily, and my mother's family came here from Naples. They came to America for a better life, and they worked hard to achieve the American dream as do all immigrants. Whenever I speak with people who have come here from other countries, they are incredulous as to what is happening here. They tell me that the violence and burning of police cars and buildings they are seeing play out in some of our big cities is reminiscent of what they left behind—a sad commentary.

One of my poems come to mind, and it seems appropriate to share it here:

My New Land

As I gazed long ago, across the sea,
My mind's eye glimpsed a new land for me.
So I left my land to go far away
In search of freedom, come what may—
To put down roots, to search for love,
To freely worship God above.
The days were long and very lonely.
Hard work and prayer were oft my only
refuge from my daily strife.
I turned to him when things got tough, and
there always seemed to be enough
to make it through my weary life.
I reached my goal, and I am blessed!
I found my love, achieved my quest.
America is home to me and to
my cherished family.
America, to have and hold,
In my new land, will I grow old.

As Americans, we must never take for granted the wonderful land we live in or the freedom and quality of life we enjoy. We must also be mindful of the poor and marginalized in our society and their needs. As a God-fearing people, we know we have a scriptural mandate to take care of one another. We must also be cognizant of the fact that we are responsible for protecting our rights by electing people to office that will fight to protect these rights.

I am heartened and thankful for all the faithful who are committed to these principles. The evangelicals stood together for candidate Trump in 2016, and thank God, we did! We must do it again in 2020. Believers, don't shy away from what we believe. We feel it is our duty and obligation to evangelize and share the good news of the Bible to all who are open to it. Immigrants, cherish all our liberties, but high on the list is our right to vote and the right to worship God without censor.

All Americans I believe are committed to voting in November. I know I will once again be voting for President Trump who stands up for religious liberty and the Christian-Judeo principles our country was founded upon as well as for the policies that are keeping us out of war and at peace. As a matter of fact, President Trump just presided over the signing of peace treaties between Bahrain and Israel and the United Arab Emirates and Israel called the Abraham Accords. This is a historic and landmark initiative for peace in the Middle East. It is reported that other Arab nations will follow suit. The world is hopeful that peace will eventually prevail between Israel and Palestine. As a result, President Trump was nominated for four Nobel Peace Prizes—the first for the Abraham Accord and the second for his peace initiative between Kosovo and Serbia and for keeping us out of wars. President Trump is the first president to receive four nominations for the coveted Nobel Peace Prize in his one term of office—an admirable record of foreign policy achievements. However, the mainstream media, social media, and most news organizations have ignored these achievements. We have seen our president fight for us his whole term, and he is winning in spite of the opposition and attacks he receives nonstop by the Leftist Democrat Party and mainstream media. This is evidenced by the Democrats' desperate attempts to overthrow him.

We are all searching for purpose and meaning in our lives regardless of our religious affiliation. I believe that it is faith—the belief in a higher power—and prayer that gives us peace, hope, and strength when we need it most. The Bible teaches us that it is our responsibility to love the Lord and to love and serve one another. Jesus said, "The greatest commandment is this: 'You shall love the Lord your God with all your heart, and with all your soul, and with all your mind.' This is the great and first commandment; and a second is like it: 'You shall love your neighbor as yourself'" (Matthew 22:37–39, Revised American Standard Version, American Bible Society). It is easy to love God. The people that hate us and try to hurt us, not so much. All we can do is pray for them, their conversion, and their change of heart.

I pray daily for an end to the hatred and attacks on our faith and religious freedom and the violence in our cities. Liberal leaders tell us we cannot worship in church because of COVID-19. They insist that we must adhere to social distancing restrictions. However, the shoulder-to-shoulder protests go unchallenged by them. The hypocrisy is staggering, but our religious leaders and pastors are resilient. They began early on livestreaming masses and religious services.

Since then, President Trump has determined that religious services and worship are essential. This was a successful effort to thwart the restrictions on our religious liberty by the radical Socialist Democrat political leaders. We are blessed to have someone fighting for us against the tyranny of the Left. The COVID-19 pandemic provided the excuse to limit our liberties, and the Liberal political leaders have taken full advantage of it.

I become more fearful every day. I am addicted to listening to the news and at the same time hesitant to turn on the television set. We are watching unimaginable sights on our television screens of cities being burned and looted, statues being torn down, people killed, and law enforcement officers injured or killed. It is not only heartbreaking; it is just plain frightening. To make matters worse and what is more disgusting is how the Liberal city and state leaders are preventing law enforcement officers from defending themselves. This is anathema to me! The police and law enforcement officers are under unprecedented attack. We are starting to see the fallout from that, but they are still being unsupported by the Democrat mayors and governors.

Lately, I find myself fighting panic attacks and anxiety more often. It seems to come about after I've watched the news. It all looks like a very bad movie or a nightmare. I wish it were a nightmare. That way, I would wake up and my America would once again be how I knew her. I keep praying. I know prayer is powerful and that many Americans are praying with me. That helps.

The agenda of the Democrat Party, in action for decades through their policies of welfare and entitlements, have kept the poor, poor for years. Teenage pregnancies leading to single, one-parent families exacerbate the problem. It is a cycle of poverty. The other by-product is the fatherless society it creates. Seventy percent of Black families are fatherless. This has led to increased crime and hopelessness. It is a vicious cycle. The cycle needs to be broken; the poor need a way out. Better education and school choice are a good place to start. They also need to know that Socialism will make their lives worse, not better.

The *New York Times* the 1619 Project is an ongoing and interactive project developed in 2019 and directed by Nikole Hannah-Jones, a reporter for the *New York Times*. The project "aims to reframe the country's history by placing the consequences of slavery and the contributions of Black Americans at the very center of the United States national narrative." The project was timed for the four hundredth anniversary of the arrival of the first enslaved Africans in the Virginia colony in 1619 and suggests this date represents the "nation's birth year."

All people are beginning to see the reality of the Socialist Democrat agenda, especially African Americans. Ironically, how many Black Democrats know the history of the party as the party of slavery? I didn't know that until I heard it and researched it.

President Trump campaigned on breaking that cycle of poverty. He not only was successful in growing the economy but he was instrumental in effecting the lowest unemployment numbers for African Americans, Latinos, Asians, and all demographics. President Trump has also followed through by enacting prison reform and opportunity zones. Although we are beginning to see signs of economic recovery, the stock market is near where it was prior to the pandemic. The economy, thanks to a strong foundation, is coming back, although our gross domestic product (GDP) is down a scary 32.9 percent on August 3, 2020.

Unemployment is coming back more slowly because people are still filing for benefits. According to Fox News, on August 7, 2020, July saw a drop of unemployment to 10.2 percent, as the US adds 1.8 million jobs. In August, the rate dropped to 8.4 percent with an addition of 1.4 million more jobs to the economy. Good news!

The year 2020 will be remembered as sad, scary, and probably the most challenging year of the century. We have had to endure so many challenges, seemingly all at once. We have lived through impeachment hearings, the COVID-19 pandemic, and the attempt by the Left to take away our freedoms. One by one, our rights are being taken away from us, and like sheep following blindly, we remain silent.

"Since the earliest days of our youth, we have been conditioned to accept that the direction of the herd, and authority anywhere—is always right" (Suzy Kassem). History has many quotes of the herd mentality phenomenon, and it is worth the time it takes to research this. There is *always* a tragic result for the people that fall for this manipulation.

Why are people so easily manipulated? I believe that people can be manipulated when they are frightened. We were so fearful of this virus that we did as we were told without question. We put our trust in politicians, the governors that closed our schools, our businesses, and our churches. We listened with laser focus, as the "medical experts" and scientists gave us models of infection and death to the tune of two and half million deaths in our country alone!

We saw Governor Cuomo of New York and others give the order for nursing homes to accept COVID-19 patients, killing thousands of elderly nursing home and assisted-living residents. There is an investigation underway, along with many lawsuits by grieving families.

The left-wing news media bombard us with misinformation, doing their best to spread panic and uncertainty. They were all wrong! So that begs the question, "What was their goal?" This is not a biblical issue; this is a rights issue! The real goal is to destroy the economy, jobs, manufacturing, and all the successes of the Trump administration. So why don't we fight back? How do we fight back?

Our country is at a crossroads. We cannot afford to stand idly by and watch as our nation is being torn apart by those who would destroy us. We have an opportunity to save our country, to take back our rights, and to take back control of our destiny. That opportunity will come on November 3, 2020. We have a choice between freedom, liberty, Capitalism, and free enterprise or Socialism and a Totalitarian government that will continue to take away our freedom. A government controlled by the people or the people controlled by the government. Globalists, the left-wing mainstream media, and the radical Socialist Democrats are desperately trying to lead us down a path to Socialism and eventually Communism. It is time for *us* to be woke.

On September 29, 1959, Nikita Khrushchev said this:

> Your children's children will live under communism. You Americans are so gullible. No, you won't accept communism outright. But we will keep feeding you small doses of socialism until you will finally wake up and find you already have communism. We will not have to fight you. We will so weaken your economy, until you will fall like overripe fruit into our hands.

"The democracy will cease to exist when you take away from those who are willing to work and give to those who are not." Sound familiar?

As incredible as it sounds, that is what the Socialist Democrat Party have in store for us if we elect them in November. The first thing Biden promised to do was to raise taxes and begin working on his promise to "transform" our country.

This book will be out long after the election, I'm afraid, but Americans will see the fruits of their decisions, either way, in short order. It won't take long.

So how do you create a Socialistic state?

* Control healthcare and you control the people.
* Increase the poverty level as high as possible. Poor people are easier to control and will not fight back if you are providing everything for them.
* Increase the debt to an unsustainable level. That way, you are able to increase taxes which will produce more poverty.
* Gun control. Remove the ability to defend themselves from the government and you will be able to create a police state.
* Welfare. Take control of every aspect (food, housing, income) of their lives because that will make them fully dependent on the government.
* Education. Take control of what people read and listen to and take control of what children learn in school.
* Religion. Remove belief in God from the government and schools so as to lead people to believe in *only* the government knowing what is best for them.
* Class warfare. Divide the people into the wealthy and the poor. Eliminate the middle class. This will cause more discontent. Therefore, it will be easier to tax the wealthy with the support of the poor.

If our republic and democracy are to be saved, Americans must first be made aware, if they are not already. Then unite to fight this scourge and attack on our country and our way of life. Fight back, America!

My father always taught me to beware of the word "free." Nothing is free, he told us, not even our freedom. Too many men and women have fought and died for it.

I believe the younger generation is being taken in by the Green New Deal initiative of the radical Left. They are right to want a clean environment; we all do. If they did the research, they would find that America has the cleanest air in the world, and it has even improved in the past decade. While we do have issues that need to be constantly addressed, it is the rest of the world that is contributing the most to the pollution of our planet. The Green New Deal being proposed by the radical Socialist Democrats will not only cost more but will use more fossil fuel to achieve their goals. People need to do the research and the math instead of being blindly led down this destructive path.

California, Oregon, and Washington State are experiencing the burning of millions of acres from wildfires out of control. Liberals say it is happening because of climate change. Environmentalists have been saying for years that it is because forest management has been restricted by Liberal laws from taking down rotted, dried, and dead trees and leaves. Environmental activists lobbied for these restrictions and had those laws passed. It doesn't take a genius to figure out how to remedy this. We need new laws. We need to cull the dead trees from the forests. "Sheep only need a single flock, but people need two, one to belong to and make them feel comfortable, and another to blame all of society's problems on" (James Rozoff).

The young people are also attracted to the idea of tuition-free education, the elimination of existing student loans, free health care for all including illegal immigrants, and open borders as promised by the radical Socialist Democrats.

In the countries where Socialism and Communism exist, the younger generation was easier to convince and control for several reasons:

1. They are idealistic and believe the propaganda of the Left. They are altruistic and well-meaning. However, they are programmed by their professors and the Left to distrust the government and our history. They won't realize until too late that a Socialist government will continue to take away their freedoms until the government eventually controls them.

2. They want to believe the propaganda that promises free college and education, health care for all, and so on. But who do they think will pay for all of this? They are being told that only the "billionaires" will pay. They will find out for themselves that the middle class will also pay. The money has to come from somewhere. The fact is that it will come from raising taxes. They will, in time, realize that all

citizens will pay dearly, *including them*. They will learn that nothing is free.

3.   They are not taking into consideration the loss of their freedom, partially because it is happening slowly. Freedom of speech is already being threatened and, in some cases, taken away. Too many of them have been indoctrinated by Liberal teachers and professors who have prevented them from voicing their opinions or expressing independent thought and ideas. Even if they wanted to speak up, they do not; they are afraid of the repercussions of doing so. Unfortunately, that is the case even in some workplaces today.

4.   They will find out—and I hope not the hard way—that if you get everything from the government, the government then owns you.

Ironically, the COVID-19 pandemic has exposed the Liberal Socialist agenda for what it is. I know from speaking to millennials in my own family that they are not happy about the freedoms taken away from them due to the coronavirus. They, like the rest of us, were forced to stay in. The bars and restaurants, gyms, beaches, and favorite hangouts were locked down. Sports events and games were canceled until further notice. Many lost their jobs or were furloughed. Limiting their freedom of speech was one thing, but not being able to go out with friends, a sudden elimination of their social life, was quite another. I hope this gives them a glimpse of what Socialism is really like. As my father used to say, "A word to the wise is sufficient." I hope so.

We all realize, or at least we pray, that this is a temporary situation. We know for sure though that a Socialist state is permanent. Life, as we know it, will never be the same if, God forbid, that ever came to pass.

Just look at Venezuela. Venezuela was one of the richest, if not the richest, countries in South America. Their path to Socialism began with a cultural revolution that saw protesters take down statues, burn public and private buildings and property, and take over the government and law enforcement. Next, they confiscated all the weapons of the citizens. Any of this sound familiar? Dissenters and protesters have been and continue to be arrested and, in some cases, executed. They are unable to defend themselves. The poor people of Venezuela are starving. They lack food, medicine, and most essentials while the dictator, Nicolas Maduro, has pocketed billions of dollars which he has stashed in foreign bank accounts. Venezuela is sitting on a large oil supply, but the people are struggling to find gasoline. This is the reality of Socialism. *Nothing* is free! There is a huge price to pay, starting with your freedom and liberty.

Communist China is another example. Does anyone remember Tiananmen Square? The Tiananmen Square protests were student-led demonstrations calling for democracy, free speech, and free press. The students also argued that China's education system did not adequately prepare them for an economic system with elements of free markets and Capitalism. They were halted by a bloody crackdown by the Chinese Communist Party on June 4 and 5, 1989, known as the Tiananmen Square Massacre.

In 2018, Communist China put more than one hundred thousand of their Uighur citizens in hard labor camps. Uighurs are a Muslim minority. My heart broke when I saw the scenes on the news of these poor people, all with shaved heads so you could not tell if they were men or women, young or old. They were kneeling on the ground in the train yard, shackled and blindfolded. One million have been imprisoned in camps according to Bahram Sintash.

Hong Kong citizens were protesting against China for taking away the freedoms they have long enjoyed until the Chinese take-over. However, China is succeeding in squelching these protests.

The free world can do nothing but look on with dismay. This is the reality of Socialism and Communism. This is the reality of a Totalitarian, one-party regime. Thank God, the Constitution of the United States, Declaration of Independence, and Bill of Rights protect us.

We now have our Second Amendment right. The Second Amendment of our Constitution protects American citizens. It reads: *"Right to bear arms.* A well-regulated militia, being necessary to the security of a *free state*, and the right of the people to keep and bear arms *shall not* be infringed." [emphasis added]

These are currently our rights. Will we fight to keep them? Does it have to come to that? All Americans should read and familiarize themselves with our Constitution.

The Constitution of the United States:

> Preamble: We, the people of the United States, in order to form a more perfect Union, establish justice, ensure domestic tranquility, provide for the common defense, promote general welfare, and secure the blessings of liberty to ourselves and our posterity, do ordain and establish this Constitution for the United States of America.

Our Constitution is in stark contrast to the evils of Socialism and Communism (and Globalism, which is the euphemism commonly used by Globalists and Leftists today).

The attack on our freedom has been silently going on for many decades, but the outright attack began with the murder of George Floyd. On May 25, 2020, the brutal murder of George Floyd—an African American man in the custody of a police officer in Minneapolis, Minnesota—exploded into protests that escalated into riots and looting across our country. Everyone agrees that this murder was a despicable act of violence on the part of the police officer. Minneapolis's radical answer to this tragedy? Abolish the police department in their city altogether. Isn't that like throwing the baby out with the bathwater? The city council has voted to eliminate the police force but has learned that the city charter calls for the city to maintain a police force. They are in the process of rewriting the charter. How absurd! How radical can you get? Who will keep the peace? Will the citizens really accept this?

On September 18, 2020, a high school senior was shot and killed. The community is beginning to see the light. They are angry and frightened. The principal of the Patrick Henry High School spoke up and told reporters that the community wants good law enforcement. The city of Minneapolis is out of control.

In Atlanta, Georgia, Rayshard Brooks was shot and killed by a police officer while he was resisting arrest. He struggled with the police officer, stole the officer's stun gun, and shot the stun gun at the officer while running away. The police officer is claiming self-defense. The videos submitted seem to support this, but time will tell. In the meantime, the officer was immediately fired and charged with murder. I might add he was charged without a grand jury and before the investigation was concluded. The Wendy's restaurant in Atlanta, Georgia, where this occurred, was burned to the ground, and a young girl, standing with her mom, was killed by a stray bullet.

The fatalities by those police officers caused widespread protests and riots across the country. Cities were looted and businesses burned to the ground. More people died, including police and innocent citizens murdered by the anarchists.

Peaceful protests for change, for police reform, and for enhanced training is understandable. Rioting, murder, and the destruction of our cities is not.

Bills were written and sent to Congress for police reform, but the Democrats would not even send it to the floor for debate, discussion of amendments, or compromise. It seems they would rather have the issue for the coming election than the solution. Once again, President Trump took action and signed an executive order for police reform.

Peaceful protesters were exercising their right, according to our First Amendment, for peaceful assembly. However, these peaceful protests were hijacked by extremist groups, anarchists, and agitators, namely Antifa and Black Lives Matter. These anarchists turned the peaceful protests into riots, arson, looting, and destruction of property and businesses in major cities of the United States. Private citizens trying to protect their homes, stores, and businesses were attacked, injured, and, in some cases, murdered.

Shocking as this sounds, or maybe not, if we look back on all the outlandish lies told by Democrats, Congressman Jerry Nadler said during a television news interview that Antifa "is a myth." In the first debate with President Trump, Biden stated that Antifa was "an idea," not an organization. Reminds me of that old saying, "Do you believe me or your eyes?" I don't know about you, but I believe my own eyes. This "myth" or "idea" is burning down our cities in an effort to destroy our democracy.

At the time of this writing, over seven hundred police officers were injured, disabled, and many have been killed since the peaceful protests, looting, and riots began. Just recently, two sheriff officers were ambushed while sitting in their patrol car in California. Thankfully, they are expected to survive. The African American shooter is still at large.

Thousands of police officers have resigned to date, and many are calling in sick and not going to work—a phenomenon called the blue flu. They are demoralized, and understandably upset, that their respective Liberal mayors and governors do not stand behind them. Liberal Democrat leaders have called for the defunding of police departments. To clarify, defunding does not mean taking away their salaries, but it does mean taking away money for items that support their work. As in all budgets, some moneys can and should be cut to minimize wasteful spending, but this should be looked at closely. I doubt, given his track record, that Mayor De Blasio gave this any thought. De Blasio called for taking $1 billion from the police budget. The city council approved the measure in mid-June. Crime in the city is skyrocketing. Consequently, New York City is on the way to becoming a shell of the great city it was. It looks like a ghost town! People that can afford it are leaving in droves, and many police are filing for early retirement or resigning.

One of my friends has a client who is a police union leader in New Jersey. The family lives in South Jersey, and their children attend a private parochial school. In conversation with the school principal, it was learned that he is getting many requests to tour his school from New Yorkers, mostly from Tribeca. When he asked one of the parents why, they told him that they decided they would sell their apartment in Tribeca and change residency from New York to New Jersey so that their children could attend a parochial or private school here. It seems that only the poor are staying in the city due to the fact that they cannot afford to move. Coincidental? While the exodus from New York continues, the real estate market has been booming in New Jersey and Florida. Way to go, Governor Cuomo. Pretty soon, the entire state of New York may be a ghost town. Lawlessness is overtaking the city due to the failed leadership of Mayor De Blasio, who blames it all on the pandemic. Seriously?

According to Fox News on August 4, 2020, "New York City Health Commissioner Dr. Oxiris Barbot resigned from her post Tuesday, citing Mayor Bill De Blasio's handling of the coronavirus pandemic in a critical letter." De Blasio confirmed that he received her resignation letter and quickly appointed Dr. Dave A. Choksi as her replacement.

As I mentioned earlier, some radical Democrat political leaders are even going a step further, advocating to abolish the police departments in their cities altogether. As a matter of fact, I just learned from the news today that one-third of the Minneapolis police force are submitting resignations and will be gone by December 2020. Residents are being told by police that, in the future, should they dial 9-1-1 they may just get a recording. What are the citizens supposed to do then? Time will tell how all this will turn out, but it doesn't look good right now.

Common sense should tell us that abolishing our police forces is not in anyone's best interest. Increasing crime and lawlessness is never the answer. It not only leads to the decline of our cities and communities but the quality of life for its citizens. It is already happening. Homicides are increasing exponentially.

In Chicago alone, homicides have risen 139 percent compared to 2019, and that is only seven months ago! What the percentage will be in December, I wonder. On Saturday, July 4, Natalia Wallace was shot to death while playing in her grandmother's backyard. She was only seven years old! Also shot and killed was a fourteen-year-old boy along with four others in the Englewood neighborhood on Chicago's south side, and another seven-year-old girl was killed in Austin. Later in the month, the carnage in Chicago took the lives of a twenty-month-old baby and a ten-year-old girl. They were among fourteen deaths in one weekend alone, and still, the violence continues. By the way, once again, Black Lives Matter was nowhere to be found. Their silence is deafening!

Most Americans appreciate and respect our police and feel safe knowing that the police are there to protect us. We feel safe knowing that if, God forbid, we need to dial 9-1-1 someone will answer and the police will come to our aid. But if these Liberal mayors and governors get their way and abolish their police forces, what then? I have a question, "Who should we call if and when we need help?" The Liberal mayor? The governor? The fire department? The protesters? No more 9-1-1? This is insanity! Are there some bad apples? Yes, and they should be held accountable, but 99 percent of these people are brave officers of the law that put their lives on the line for us every day. In fact, they are the front line for the safety of our communities.

On September 22, 2020, Louisville, Kentucky, erupted in protests after a grand jury indicted one of three officers in the shooting death of Breonna Taylor during a drug raid six months ago. During the second night of protests, two police officers were shot. The suspect is in custody. Thank God, they are so far in stable condition.

The fact that law enforcement and police officers in general are under attack not just figuratively but literally should scare the heck out of all Americans. We are hearing that these mobs are now expanding their violence from the business communities into the suburbs. Couple that with the reduction in police protection and we must ask ourselves, "Who will keep us safe?" We are under attack on many fronts, and we want it to end, but it seems the deep state and left-wing Socialist Democrat politicians are so hell-bent on removing President Trump from office that the destruction of our cities seems to be of no concern to them. They don't seem to care about the economy, keeping the peace, immigration, our First and Second Amendment rights, or our very democracy. Their hatred of Donald Trump and their quest for power is what drives them. Their hatred of our president is visceral, and I believe there are two main reasons. First being that he is the only one standing in the way of their goal to "transform" our country into a Socialist, Totalitarian system of government and their Progressive Liberal agenda.

As a matter of fact, former vice president Joe Biden, the Democrat Party nominee who will run against President Trump in the November 2020 election, said as much again in an interview in July. He said, if elected president, he will raise taxes and "transform this country." Another example of evil telling you what they want to do. To be fair, Biden is now saying—in August 2020 interview—that he will raise taxes on people that make $400,000 or more and not on the middle class.

We all know that once taxes are raised on the rich, everyone is vulnerable to having their taxes raised, especially if the radical Democrats get their way on entitlements. Former vice president Biden continues to say whatever it takes to appease his base and often contradicts himself.

The second motivation is the Supreme Court. The Democrat Party is apoplectic; their hair is on fire because it seems there is little to stand in the way of President Trump nominating a third Supreme Court justice in his first term and probably getting his nominee confirmed by the Senate as is his right and obligation as president of the United States according to the Constitution.

I believe—and pray—that these policies will backfire on Democrats in November. They may be starting to realize that their constituents are beginning to blame them for the current civil unrest and the violence and murders that are taking place due to their inaction.

Anarchists took over six city blocks in Seattle, Washington. They barricaded the perimeters, and armed thugs stood guard, refusing to admit police or law enforcement into the occupied area. They have declared themselves an "autonomous zone" separate from the rest of the country. They initially called themselves CHAZ, short for Capitol Hill Autonomous Zone. They have since decided that they will be called Capitol Hill Organized Protest or CHOP. These anarchists have extorted money from local businesses within this boundary supposedly for "protection." They have even barred people from entering their own homes. They refuse to leave unless their demands are met. These include disbanding the police department, giving free college for all citizens, emptying prisons, and more.

Incredibly, the mayor of Seattle has called the protests and occupation a "summer of love" and nothing more than a "street festival." This was contradicted when the so-called "street festival" turned violent, ending in the shooting and death of two African American teenagers. Horace Lorenzo Anderson was shot and killed. He had recently graduated from high school. Another man is in critical condition in the hospital. Another sixteen-year-old died, and a fourteen-year-old is in intensive care. The police arrived to investigate and begged to be allowed in to help the victims but were turned away by an angry armed mob of occupying thugs. Could that young man have been saved? We will never know. The aforementioned mayor of Seattle has made an about-face since a group of protesters was led to her home, threatening her and her family and covering her home with graffiti. She is now claiming the shootings and violence are against the law. Weren't they against the law a week before when Horace Lorenzo Anderson and others were killed?

On July 1, 2020, Mayor Durkin signed an executive order at three o'clock in the morning calling the CHOP unlawful. Since the occupation of her city began, there have been four shootings, two deaths—both teenagers, sixty-five robberies, assaults, and many injuries, not to mention the destroyed businesses. Yet it took her home being threatened to act in the middle of the night. It looks like fear and violence hit too close to home for Mayor Durkin. She has announced that the police will be able to move back into their precinct. That has not yet happened. As a matter of fact, it is still under siege. When her executive order was signed, the chief of police sent in armed police in riot gear and armored vehicles to clear the area. Many arrests were made, and the cleanup of the community began, but that did not last. Thanks to her initial support of the occupation and her inaction, this armed protest has evolved into a dangerous confrontation with law enforcement. She has put many lives in danger and cost many business owners lost revenue at the least and total loss at most as well as the destruction of their properties.

Emboldened by the Liberal Democrat leaders' do-nothing approach, more and more armed thugs and anarchists are rioting and looting in other large cities. One would think that the Liberal Democrat leaders would learn from what happened in Seattle. Not so. Sadly, it seems their only goal is to defeat President Trump in the November election at any cost. Even at the cost of our great cities.

The Justice Department and law enforcement are not off the hook either. They also did not take action until recently. Attorney General Bill Barr put together a task force to handle the civil unrest and lawlessness. He promised that arrests would be made.

What is happening in America today? If we continue to ignore what is happening before our eyes, we will surely lose. It will become too late. I know it has been said before, but it is true now more than ever—our vote has never been more important.

I can recall when some of the celebrities in Hollywood said that they would move out of the country if Donald Trump was elected president. He was, and they didn't. I wonder, just out of curiosity, where these people would have moved to. One answer, I guess, is Greece. That is where actor Tom Hanks and his wife have gone. I wish them all the best. Greece is indeed a beautiful country.

There are beautiful places in this world, but there is no place like home. There is no greater place to live than in a free America. Just ask the millions of people around the world that want to come to our country.

It is good to read the words of William Tyler Page, the patriot who reminds us of who we are as Americans:

The American Creed

I believe in the United States of America, as a government of the people, by the people, for the people; whose just powers are derived from the consent of the governed; a democracy in a republic; a sovereign nation of many sovereign states; a perfect union, one and inseparable; established upon those principles of freedom, equality, justice, and humanity for which American patriots sacrificed their lives and fortunes.

I therefore believe it is my duty to my country to love it, to support its Constitution, to obey its laws, to respect its flag, and to defend it against all enemies.

HOW DID WE GET HERE?

When I was growing up, I loved to watch movies on television. The genre that I enjoyed most as a teenager was the love stories, especially the World War II love stories. The story line was usually the wartime nurse falling in love with the wounded soldier or the boy next door either going to war or coming back from the war. As I am writing, three such movies are coming to mind, and I am smiling.

As a matter of fact, those movies are probably why I wanted to be a nurse when I grew up. Biology class put the kibosh on that idea though. I discovered I did not like the sight of blood or the idea of dissecting animals.

I decided instead to become a hairdresser. At least I would still wear the white uniform and shoes. Come to think of it, I must have really liked to wear a uniform. I went to a Catholic high school, became a hairdresser, and then joined the United States Navy!

Getting back to television shows though, my brother and I used to fight over what shows to watch especially on Saturday mornings. My brother fought tooth and nail to watch the cowboy shows and gangster movies. My mom usually had to step in and settle the issue because we only had one television set. Her solution was to compromise. So we compromised. I didn't mind though if the show was *The Lone Ranger* or *The Roy Rogers and Dale Evans Show*. I remember my brother running around the house with his cowboy hat and boots and pretend shooting at the bad guys. Unfortunately, I was sometimes the bad guy!

My brother and I both agreed on shows like *Howdy Doody, East Side Kids, Lunch with Soupy Sales, Superman*, and other popular kids' shows. I also enjoyed movies like *The Wizard of Oz* and all the Shirley Temple and Walt Disney movies. Those are good memories.

The violence we saw on TV and in the movies were the shoot-outs in the cowboy shows and gunfire in the gangster movies and murder mysteries and detective shows like *Columbo* and *Perry Mason*.

As a child, I remember reading every Nancy Drew mystery in the series. I still like to watch reruns of *Murder, She Wrote* with Angela Lansbury.

What shows we watched were mostly up to us, children. If we didn't enjoy the shoot-'em-ups, we turned the channel. Yes, we actually had to get up to switch channels. Remote controls were not available yet.

My parents watched the news in the evening and enjoyed their favorite shows. At that time, there were popular variety shows like *The Liberace Show*, *The Lawrence Welk Show*, *The Dean Martin Show*, and the popular *The Tonight Show Starring Johnny Carson*. The whole family enjoyed these as well as the comedy shows.

Some of the comedy shows I loved watching were *The Red Skelton Show*, *The Bob Hope Show*, *The Milton Berle Show*, *The Martin and Lewis Show*, *The Burns and Allen Show*, *The Jack Benny Program*, *The Steve Allen Show*, and many more. In my opinion, that was when comedy was really funny. Juxtapose their comedy with today's obscene comedy and there is no comparison. As a matter of fact, I was watching a rerun of *The Tonight Show Starring Johnny Carson* the other night and found myself laughing out loud! I thought to myself, "I haven't laughed out loud to a comedian in years."

I have heard many people refer to cities and society in those days as "Mayberry," which of course refers to the television city of Mayberry, North Carolina, of the popular *The Andy Griffith Show*, a show depicting an innocent time.

The sitcoms of the sixties were fictional comedies, such as *I Dream of Jeannie* and *Bewitched*, and family shows, like *Father Knows Best*, *Leave It to Beaver*, *The Brady Bunch*, *Dennis the Menace*, and others.

My favorites as a teenager were *Happy Days* and *Laverne & Shirley*.

The fifties and sixties reflected an era of innocence and whole-someness that would be unrecognizable today. Sadly, some of these shows would never be allowed to air today. The values of yesterday don't match the values or, should I say, lack of values that are commonplace today. That age of innocence is long gone, and I miss it.

Thinking back to my own childhood, I see that I took our way of life for granted, as we all did, I guess. It never occurred to me how much things could change. We thought the American way of life as we knew it would remain the same. What we weren't aware of was the insidious poison of "Liberalism" that was slowly creeping into our society. A little at a time, our way of life was changing and being corrupted, and we hardly noticed. I am aware that, as children and teenagers, we were not politically savvy. We were, for the most part, ignorant of the political and social issues being addressed in our country at that time. We were naive, at least I was.

In grammar school, we had fire drills and were taught to leave the building in an orderly manner. We also had air-raid drills. Those always scared me and fascinated me at the same time. When we heard the alarm, we had to immediately sit underneath our desks. The teacher instructed us not to look outside the window. In a real air-raid drill, we were taught never to look toward the light. She also told us that if it were a real air-raid, we would have to go into the basement to the gymnasium. Those drills were the result of the Cold War with the USSR (Union of Soviet Socialist Republics). Civil rights, women's rights, and the wars in Korea and Vietnam were in the forefront in the fifties and sixties.

The fifties brought us rock and roll. Elvis Presley got his break in the music business in the fifties. Elvis appeared on *The Ed Sullivan Show* in 1957 and was filmed only from the waist up so as not to show his gyrations. As his popularity grew that changed.

The sixties was the era of free love, flower children, peace signs, drugs, protests, and sit-ins against the war in Vietnam. It was the "hippie generation" and the era of Woodstock, concerts, and controversial songs on the hit parade. We all welcomed the British invasion with the introduction of the British bands and the Beatles in 1964.

The war in Vietnam was a turning point for this country. Young adults and celebrities lobbied and protested for peace. Some young men went to Canada to avoid the draft. Some enlisted in the military branch that they chose, rather than be drafted into the army. It was a time of change, a time of rebellion. The Vietnam War ended in 1975 and cost the lives of fifty-eight thousand servicemen.

Many of those who protested and rebelled against the Vietnam War and the establishment later became the "Liberal" teachers and professors who were just as intent on indoctrinating their Liberal ideology to their students, as the subjects they were hired to teach them. Others ran for office and became our elected mayors, congressmen, and senators. Some, thirty and forty years later, are still in office.

The movement started in the early 1900s and boiled over in the sixties, carrying us unsuspecting to a future that would threaten our Constitution and our freedom and liberty today.

The Democrat Party, through its history, has been less pro-American than anti-American. It has always been Progressive, Liberal, and anti-Semitic. The Democrat Party was also the party of slavery.

President Woodrow Wilson served as our twenty-eighth president from 1913 to 1921. He was a member of the Democratic Party and a segregationist. His statue stood in front of Princeton University in Princeton, New Jersey, where he served as president of the university and the thirty-fourth governor of New Jersey before winning the 1912 presidential election. He left a complex legacy that included resegregating many branches of the federal workforce. He wrote a textbook praising the Confederacy and, in particular, the Ku Klux Klan. He pursued an ambitious agenda of Progressive reform that included the establishment of the Federal Reserve and Federal Trade Commission. He led the country through World War I. His father served as a chaplain in the Confederate army and used his church as a hospital for Confederate troops. As president, he rolled back hard-fought economic progress for Black Americans. The statue in front of Princeton University has recently been removed citing his segregationist policies.

The taking down of all statues, including religious statues, was rampant for a while. We are fortunate that we have a president in Donald J. Trump who is determined to stem the tide of the anarchy that is trying so hard to overtake us.

Before the invention of social media, newspapers and television were the vehicles that gave us the news of the day. So much has changed.

When I was growing up, we spent a lot of time outdoors, riding our bikes, roller-skating, jumping rope, or playing ball in the playground. If our parents could afford it, we went to dancing school, music lessons, or martial arts. In my case, I remember coming home from school, changing clothes, and going out to play. We lived across the street from the elementary school, so we had a playground and ball field at our disposal. I was never good at sports, so I preferred to ride my bike or roller-skate with my friends. My brother and his friends spent time on the playground playing ball or shooting hoops.

My mother worked, so we didn't see her until we went home for dinner. My dad worked nights in the post office, slept during the day, and worked a second, part-time job as a painter on weekends. In spite of my dad's work schedule, our family always managed to have dinner together. Dad left for work after dinner and came home from work before breakfast.

I remember that we had a lot of freedom in those days. We always knew it was time to come home for dinner when we heard my dad's familiar whistle. It also became the signal for all the kids in the neighborhood to go home. They were told by their parents that when Mr. Colli whistled, they should also go home for dinner. We always marveled at how loud that whistle was. It seemed wherever we were in the neighborhood, it was heard loud and clear. We could never say we were late because we didn't hear that whistle. Well, maybe we could say that, but Dad wouldn't believe us, so we didn't bother to try. Even writing about it makes me nostalgic for those happy and uncomplicated days. At least they were uncomplicated from our point of view as children.

I'm sure many adults, including my parents, would have quite another perspective. Generally speaking, though, it was an easier time, a good era to have lived through. They were happy days, carefree days, and I am thankful to have experienced them. It was easy to be naive because so much was kept from us. As I said, there was no social media and only the news at night. There was only the innocence of our childhood. We did as we were told, and we were only told what the grown-ups thought we needed to know.

In my family, when my parents and grandparents spoke in Italian, I knew the conversation was for adults only. It is a very different story for kids today. Today there is cable TV and the Internet. The news and cable news shows are on TV nonstop. Very little is hidden or can be hidden from children's eyes and ears today. I don't know of a child who doesn't have a cell phone. They are constantly bent over their phone, texting their friends. Today it is less talking and more texting, which is hard for me to understand because by the time I get done texting, I could be finished with a conversation already! Texting removes the personal communication; it is colder and more sterile in my opinion. I guess emojis are meant to soften the text message and add some emotion and feeling.

There are different tech devices and video games that kids can play electronically with friends. There is not much in the way of outdoor activities unless they are involved in sports at school and going to the pool to swim in the summertime, although since the pandemic bicycles have become more popular with everyone. Again, the personal communication is limited.

It makes me sad because they don't even know what they are missing. They are missing the opportunity to spend more time playing outdoors and the personal interaction that is so important for the social aspect of their lives. That is exacerbated today by COVID-19 which is denying the social experience of going to school.

We in my generation—that is, people born between 1946 and 1964—are referred to as baby boomers. We are considered the generation responsible for all the huge innovations, inventions, and world-changing accomplishments of the twentieth century.

The year 1945 was the culmination of the Manhattan Project which created the atomic bomb. Before his death, President Franklin Delano Roosevelt never told his vice president, Harry Truman, about the top-secret project. When President Truman heard about the Manhattan Project for the first time after he took office, he was shocked. He had little time to catch up; there was a war on, and he found himself with a very difficult decision to make. He could decide to invade Japan, which would have lengthened the war by one to two years and possibly cost one million more lives, or he could decide to drop the atomic bomb on Japan, which he thought would immediately end World War II. We all know what he finally decided. My parents got married that year when my father came back from the war.

The Korean War began in 1950 and ended in 1953. This was the first military action of the Cold War. It was a brutal war that cost the lives of some 54,260 soldiers. Some called it "the Forgotten War" for the lack of attention it received compared to World War I, World War II, and the Vietnam War. There is still no official truce, and the peninsula remains divided.

In 1961, America had just started the space program, and President John F. Kennedy said he would like to land humans on the moon. On July 16, 1969, that dream was realized when Apollo 11 blasted off with astronauts Neil Armstrong, Edwin "Buzz" Aldrin, and Michael Collins on board. Four days later on July 20, 1969, the lunar module, the *Eagle*, landed on the moon with Neil Armstrong and Buzz Aldrin. Michael Collins stayed aboard Apollo 11 and orbited the moon. Neil Armstrong became the first human to walk on the moon where he proudly planted our American flag. On July 24, 1969, Apollo 11 came back to Earth safely. Sadly, President Kennedy did not live to see his dream realized. He was assassinated on November 22, 1963.

The decade of the seventies was a tumultuous one. It was the time of the Watergate Hotel break-in which precipitated the demise of President Nixon's presidency. President Nixon resigned in disgrace on August 9, 1974. He was later pardoned by his successor, President Gerald Ford.

The war in Vietnam that began in 1955 finally ended in 1975. All wars are terrible, but because I was in the United States Navy from 1965 to 1968, the Vietnam War impacted me in a personal way. My cousin died in Vietnam at the young age of nineteen. My brother joined the marines and spent a tour of duty there, and I met my former husband when he came back from Vietnam.

The eighties brought us President Reagan, who would go down in history as the president who saw the fall of the Berlin Wall. On June 12, 1987, President Ronald Reagan delivered his famous Berlin Wall Speech. The speech called for the general secretary of the Communist Party of the Soviet Union, Mikhail Gorbachev, to open the Berlin Wall. His famous key line in the middle of the speech was "Mr. Gorbachev, tear down this wall!" That would go down in history as one of the most quoted and memorable lines of Reagan's presidency.

The year 1991 saw the end of the USSR. The Union of Soviet Socialist Republics was broken up and became known as Russia once again.

These past decades changed the dynamics of our world and have impacted America in many unalterable ways. September 11, 2001, was the darkest day experienced by America since the Attack on Pearl Harbor. It brought on the war in Afghanistan and the war against Al-Qaeda and ISIS (Islamic State of Iraq and Syria). The ISIS caliphate has been defeated during the Trump administration, and the terror attacks have stopped—I pray—for good, but it is uncertain and, I believe, contingent on who wins the election in November. To his credit, President Trump has made sure that the two important terrorist leaders have been killed and are no longer a threat to our servicemen and servicewomen and citizens.

So here we are in the second decade of the twenty-first century. Once again, the future holds much promise but also a lot of uncertainty. One thing is for sure, the United States of America needs our prayers now more than ever. No one knows what the future holds, but we must pray for our country and do what we can to keep her free.

SOME GOOD NEWS

All is not doom and gloom, although there are some days it does look that way. However, this is America, and we must take heart.

In the midst of all that is going on, there is good news on the horizon. I am heartened that law enforcement unions and organizations across the country, including New York City Police, are endorsing President Trump. I hope all Americans are taking notice.

Forgive my redundancy, but our future depends on the outcome of the election of November 3. But regardless of what happens, we are Americans. We are strong, and we will survive. Our history proves this out.

Our country has many achievements to celebrate, beginning with the restart of our space program last spring 2020. On May 31, 2020, veteran American astronauts Doug Hurley and Bob Behnken lifted off from the Kennedy Space Center in Cape Canaveral, Florida. There they boarded the Crew Dragon capsule on top of a Falcon 9 rocket. The rocket ship was designed and built by Elon Musk's SpaceX company, making it the first launch of astronauts into orbit by a private firm. It is also NASA's first human spaceflight in nearly a decade. Nineteen hours after the launch, the Crew Dragon capsule successfully joined the International Space Station, 250 miles above the Earth. One week later, the Falcon 9 rocket was launched into space again, this time unmanned but with satellites aboard. Two months later, on August 2, 2020, NASA astronauts Doug Hurley and Bob Behnken splashed down in the Gulf of Mexico in a SpaceX Crew Dragon spacecraft, ending their historic trip to space and the space station. This collaborative effort by NASA and SpaceX was a huge undertaking and a huge success. Finally, we are back in space. This is one of the most important achievements for our national security to date. NASA has landed a spacecraft on an asteroid that has been circling the universe for billions of years, and it is reported to be taking back samples to Earth. The last time a shuttle mission lifted off was on July 8, 2011, when the *Atlantis* lifted off from the Kennedy Space Center. It was the final shuttle mission when President Obama decided to end our space program.

This was a historic and monumental achievement for America and would not have been possible had President Trump not supported this effort. This was also the realization of Elon Musk's dream of putting humans in space, with the forward vision of colonizing the moon and eventually Mars.

The liftoff and docking with the International Space Station was a sight to behold. I know it brought tears to *my* eyes, and I'm certain there was a multitude of prayers and best wishes going up for those brave astronauts and the success of their mission. It was a victorious day for America!

On July 30, 2020, NASA's Mars 2020 *Perseverance* rover lifted off from Cape Canaveral, Florida, and blasted into space on its epic seven-month mission to the Red Planet. The rover launched into space atop a United Launch Alliance Atlas V rocket at 7:50 a.m., eastern daylight time, from Launch Complex 41 at Cape Canaveral Space Force Station. The journey to Mars will take seven months. The rover is scheduled to land on Mars's Jezero crater on February 18, 2021. The mission's duration on the Red Planet's surface is at least one Martian year or 687 days. A Mars helicopter is also being transported with the rover. The helicopter, called *Ingenuity*, will be the first aircraft to attempt powered flight on another planet. The *Perseverance* rover will search for evidence of ancient life on Mars.

China recently launched its own Tianwen-1 mission to land a rover on Mars, and the United Arab Emirates launched its *Amal* orbiter. It will not land on Mars but orbit the surface.

So far, the United States of America has been the only country to successfully put a spacecraft on Mars eight times. Two NASA landers, *InSight* (Interior Exploration using Seismic Investigations, Geodesy and Heat Transport) and *Curiosity*, are currently operating there. Six other spacecrafts are exploring the planet from orbit:

three from US, two from Europe, and one from India. "NASA's longer-term goal is to send a manned mission to Mars in the 2030s" (as reported by Chris Ciaccia, James Rogers, and David Aaro of Fox News and the Associated Press).

On July 8, 2011, our last shuttle mission was launched. It carried four astronauts on a twelve-day delivery mission to the International Space Station. President Obama ended our thirty-year Space Shuttle program, saying, "This is the end of an era of human spaceflight, but opens another." His vision was future space exploration, with eventual travel to Mars, but the budget was never approved by Congress. He also envisioned a "redirect asteroid" program in 2025. This is a very important program for the safety and security of our planet. It would potentially protect us from asteroids that could collide with the Earth.

As a matter of fact, a refrigerator-sized asteroid will come very close to our planet on November 2, the day before the election. It is reported that there is a good chance that it could hit us. They say that they believe there will not be too much damage. It is not known, however, exactly where it will impact the Earth. As if we don't have enough problems!

On October 20, 2020, in a daring NASA mission, NASA's OSIRIS-REx (Origins, Spectral Interpretation, Resource Identification, Security, Regolith Explorer) spacecraft has successfully reached out and touched Bennu, a tiny top-shaped asteroid that's been spinning through the solar system for a billion years. If all went as planned, the spacecraft scooped up a bit of material during its brief moment of contact and departed seconds later with its precious cargo—rocks and dust dating back to the solar system's birth (from an article by Michael Greshko).

In 2001, a congressionally appointed commission led by Defense Secretary Donald Rumsfeld envisioned the establishment of a space corps within the air force to help "avoid a space Pearl Harbor." In 2016, John Hamre, deputy secretary of defense under past president Clinton, raised the possibility of a "space service" within the air force. In 2017, US representatives Jim Cooper (Democratic Party, Tennessee) and Mike Rogers (Republican Party, Alabama) called for the creation under the secretary of the air force of a new space corps "as a separate military service." That same year, the Trump administration reopened the National Space Council. In 2018, President Trump reestablished the US Space Command.

After NATO (North Atlantic Treaty Organization) unveiled plans to recognize space as an operational domain of warfare in June 2019, France established a space command within the French air force one month later. In December 2019, Britain announced the creation of a UK space command.

The US Space Force (USSF) was born following the passage of the 2020 defense bill.

> The Space Force shall be organized, trained and equipped to provide freedom of operation for the United States in, from, and to, space; and prompt and sustained space operations... It shall be the duty of the Space Force to protect the interests of the United States in space; deter aggression in, from, and to space; and conduct space operations.

The decision to sign the 2020 National Defense Authorization Act was vitally important. Although the idea was around for many years, the credit goes to the wisdom and foresight of President Trump and his administration for making it a reality.

Most Americans do not realize how much we depend on space for communications, commerce, air and ground transport, emergency services, and, most importantly, the national security of America. The United States of America must keep its place as number 1 in space for our national security and the ultimate safety of our nation against cyber and other attacks from those that would do us harm. Maintaining the number 1 position in space will deter our enemies and protect our planet.

We, Americans, are indeed beginning to see a light at the end of the tunnel. Churches and synagogues are reopening, and we are hopeful that schools will reopen in the fall as well, although that is still up in the air due to the rise in COVID-19 cases and the plans to protect the students and teachers are still being debated.

The month of June saw the reopening of hair and nail salons, hotels, and casinos. Restaurants are opening for outdoor dining with enhanced safety protocols and limited seating for social distancing. Most states have opened earlier and are slowly returning to a new normal. However, some states are experiencing a setback with the rise of COVID-19 infections. The governors have taken a step back and have slowed down the opening of their states "for the safety of their citizens."

Families and friends are meeting together again. This was especially good news for senior citizens, who suffered the most from being separated from their loved ones, myself included. The elderly are still advised to stay in their homes for their own safety and continue to wear facial masks. They are the most vulnerable along with the autoimmune compromised and those patients with underlying health conditions, such as diabetes, heart disease, and obesity.

The rise in COVID-19 infections and the increase in hospitalizations are a real cause for concern. States most affected are reinforcing their mandates for social distancing, hygiene, and mask wearing in order to control the spread of the disease.

According to the news reports and COVID-19 briefings, this rise in cases could be attributed to a number of factors. For example, the protests across the country had thousands of protesters traveling shoulder to shoulder, obviously not social distancing and not wearing facial masks. They traveled from city to city, which makes tracking almost impossible. Young people are also letting their guard down by not wearing masks and not social distancing. They are often shown in groups and in large gatherings in parks, beaches, malls, and parties. Even though they do not have symptoms, we're told that they could still spread the disease. It is feared that is what is happening.

In spite of the rise in COVID-19 cases, the deaths are declining. Wearing masks, social distancing, and frequent handwashing are still the order of the day until a major decline in infections are seen. The infection dies without a host, so the more we distance and protect ourselves, the faster this pandemic will leave us.

The pandemic also brought us some innovations in health care, such as telemedicine. Virtual "doctor visits" using Zoom, Skype, and telephone have become the new normal. This is fast becoming a growing industry due to the pandemic and the mandate for social distancing.

Physicians are still seeing patients in person, but with very strict protocols. For example, when I made my appointment with my optometrist last week, I had to fill out the forms online and bring them with me. When I got there, I had to call the office from my cell phone, and someone came outside to let me in the building. I would not be admitted without a facial mask. I understand that is pro forma today.

How we shop will also be forever changed, but large stores like Target are hiring thousands in preparation for the holidays. Retail stores are open with very strict protocols. They are only allowing a limited amount of people to enter the store at a time to ensure social distancing, and facial masks are mandatory. Hand sanitizer is given to the shoppers and is available throughout the stores. Most stores are also taking temperatures of patrons as they enter. I have to say though that things are beginning to look better than they have.

During the pandemic, online and home shopping channels' sales are off the charts. I can personally attest to that. Amazon has geared up with thirty-three enormous distribution centers to keep up with all the online shopping. My mail carrier is delivering a lot of packages to my address lately, and I see Amazon delivery trucks everywhere!

Grocery stores and supermarkets are still doing a booming business and are also following strict protocols. I have also noticed that there is plenty of toilet paper back on the shelves, but there are rumors that it may become scarce once again. I can't, for the life of me, figure out why people are hoarding this, but it seems like a good idea to stock up again. Yikes!

The COVID-19 pandemic has shone a light on our dependence on China, India, and other countries for earth minerals, antibiotics, pharmaceuticals, and other vital products. This is not only an economical issue but a national security one as well. Consequently, we are seeing manufacturing of these products coming back to our country. We woke up just in time, thanks to President Trump.

The United States imports hydroxychloroquine from India—that is, until we were refused a much-needed shipment requested by President Trump.

According to Fortune News, on March 25, 2020, "India bans export of hydroxychloroquine amid a run on supplies globally." India has some of the world's largest manufacturers of the finished drug as well as its component ingredients, and the move is likely to crimp global supply at a time when the medication is receiving unprecedented global attention. India advocates health care workers take the drug regularly as a preventative measure.

So where did that leave us? Our health care workers required the drug for the same reason, and it is also being used as an early treatment for COVID-19 along with the antibiotic known as Z-Pak and zinc. We did manage to get a supply from other sources, but our dependence on other countries for medicine was brought to the forefront. We learned a lesson, and President Trump acted. President Trump invoked the Defense Production Act whereby companies are now manufacturing ventilators and PPE (personal protective equipment) in our country. Thankfully, there is no longer a shortage of these much-needed supplies in our country.

According to *The Wall Street Journal*, Kodak will shift into drug production with the help of $765 million loan. The funding is provided under the Defense Production Act. The Eastman Kodak Company will be manufacturing generic medications in their Tarrytown, New York, plant. This is huge, as it will loosen the US reliance on foreign sources for medications. One of the drugs that will be manufactured here is hydroxychloroquine. Unfortunately, this project is on hold for the foreseeable future because of an investigation over financing. Where did that come from? I wonder.

Forgive me for being suspicious, but hydroxychloroquine is an inexpensive drug used successfully for over seventy years, primarily for malaria but has shown great promise for COVID-19. It is being criticized and put aside for much more expensive drugs. Thankfully, it is still being used, just not publicized by the mainstream media and "experts" that stand to make a lot of money from the vaccines and therapeutics that are coming out.

Whoever thought depending on another country for lifesaving antibiotics and other medications was a good idea? Whoever it was is wrong. This pandemic is a good example of how depending on other countries, especially for medicine, is dangerous and can be life-threatening.

President Trump's intention to lower prescription drug prices by 50 to 70 percent by January 2021 represents another winning moment for our country. But yes, you guessed it. Instead of thanks, he gets resistance. Big Pharma, as he says, is "not happy with me."

Some manufacturers are resisting because not manufacturing in China will negatively impact their bottom line. I hope they are made to see the light and will put America first before profit. What are the chances of that? I wonder.

As for me, I like the sound of "made in the USA." We are told that an added benefit will be lower costs for medicines. Manufacturing more products here in America will also add to our employment numbers. More and more products are being made in the USA, thanks to President Trump. Let's hope it stays that way.

President Trump is continuing his efforts to help unemployed Americans by limiting the number of work visas from other countries. He is determined to keep jobs available for American citizens. This was good news for our workers, but he is getting the expected criticism and resistance from the "Business Round Table"—US Chamber of Commerce, Silicon Valley big tech companies, and the Liberals. What else is new? They sound like a broken record. Enough already!

Our troops are coming back from overseas. The president has recently ordered twelve thousand of our military men and women out of Germany due to Germany not paying their fair share to NATO for their defense. Some troops will be reassigned to other NATO bases and the rest deployed back home. That may change if Germany pays up. We'll see.

He is bringing our troops home from Afghanistan as well, which is another campaign promise kept.

I believe we have a lot to be thankful for and a lot to look forward to. We will get through these storms—yes, "storms," as in more than one. It looks like the COVID-19 pandemic will be with us for a while. I am hopeful that the pandemic will end, and we will have better treatments and less fatalities.

Good news on the coronavirus vaccine front! US pharmaceutical giant Pfizer has received $76 billion from the Trump administration for the development of their coronavirus vaccines. They are being manufactured in Michigan and have received "fast-track" status by the FDA (Food and Drug Administration).

Two experimental coronavirus vaccines are being jointly developed by Pfizer and German biotech firm BioNTech and Moderna. We are told that COVID-19 vaccines could be available to the public by the end of 2020 or early 2021. They are being produced by the millions so that they will be ready to be immediately deployed around the country to the most vulnerable first. Both vaccines are being produced, and the one that is deemed safe by the FDA and the scientists will be used and the others destroyed.

The country and the world were stunned in early October when it was announced that President Trump had contracted the COVID-19 coronavirus along with the first lady, Melania Trump, and their young son, Barron. President Trump was taken to Walter Reed Hospital where he was treated for three days and released back to the White House with what appears to be a miraculous recovery. The president attributes his recovery to the great care from the twelve doctors that treated him. He also credits the Regeneron antibody infusion he received as well as remdesivir and the other therapeutics. The president has given the order for the drugs given him to be given to all the hospitals and patients that request them at no charge. The first lady is recovering, and Barron is no longer symptomatic.

As for the president, he is back on the campaign trail with as many as five rallies a day in at least nine states. His energy level is remarkable. He realizes that nothing can be taken for granted and that this will be a close election although both campaigns are predicting a landslide victory. Joe Biden, on the other hand, has been rarely seen and is not being questioned by the press.

Good news! Most children are back to school! Schools are open in September in most of the country although, in some states, infections continue to rise. It is important to remember that recovery is 99 percent in people without underlying health issues or obesity and that the elderly are the most vulnerable. Hospitalizations were down at 25 percent but are now rising due to the spike in cases according to the CDC (Centers for Disease Control and Prevention).

I remain hopeful that the civil unrest and violence will end too. In the wake of the siege on some of our large cities, the Justice Department is committed to restoring law and order. However, the local Liberal political leaders are preventing their law enforcement to restore order to those cities.

The 1776 Unites project is an effort by African American historians, academics, and advocates to address alleged historical inaccuracies of the 1619 Project which was created by the *New York Times* journalist Nikole Hannah-Jones. 1776 Unites is supported by the Robert Woodson Center. In addition to material on US history and historical controversies, 1776 Unites also seeks to promote what it considers to be founding American values, like entrepreneurship, self-determination, and mutual social support. Many contributors to 1776 Unites promote current and historical examples of prosperous Black communities as "a powerful refutation of the claim that the destiny of Black Americans is determined by what whites do, or what they have done in the past." 1776 Unites also promotes the work and thought of entrepreneurs, philanthropists, business and community leaders, and others it considers "achievers," hoping to illustrate the opportunities for success that are open to African Americans today, their contributions to national economic and cultural life, and their stake in United States life and history. The efforts of the 1776 Unites project could not come at a better time for our country and for African Americans who can take pride in their achievements and successes.

Recently, President Trump has signed his own executive order for a 1776 Unites initiative to restore teaching American history and patriotism in our American schools. For too long, our history has been omitted from many curriculums with a downplay on patriotism, love of country, and respect for our American flag. Sadly, this most likely has attributed to the attitudes of many young people who feel that America is not great. This is evidenced by the young people that are joining rioters and looters who are burning down many of our great cities.

A friend recently told me her son, who was Far Left, went to visit colleges out West for different meetings and events. He was appalled at what he described as a hate of America by most students and a bent toward Communism. He came home with a totally different outlook and is done with the Left, she told me.

On September 19, 2020, Justice Ruth Bader Ginsberg passed away after a valiant battle with pancreatic cancer. Justice Ginsberg is an icon. She fought for years for women's rights issues, and she leaves a great legacy. She will lie in repose for two days at the Supreme Court and will be the first woman to lie in state at the nation's capital prior to being buried next to her husband, Martin Ginsberg, in Arlington National Cemetery. My thoughts and prayers go out to the Ginsberg family. May she rest in peace.

President Trump has announced his nominee to succeed Justice Ginsberg on Saturday, September 26, 2020. He has said it would be a woman, and so it is. President Trump has nominated Judge Amy Coney Barrett.

The four names that have been widely floated were Seventh US Court of Appeals Judge Amy Coney Barrett, Eleventh Circuit Judge Barbara Lagoa, Fourth Circuit Judge Allison Jones Rushing, and Sixth Circuit Judge Joan Larson. All have experience on the federal bench and have been through the Senate confirmation process before. Judge Amy Coney Barrett is a constitutionalist that will adhere to the law as written and is a stellar nominee.

The hearings are scheduled to begin in the Senate on October 12, 2020, and a vote did take place on October 26, 2020. Since the Republicans have the majority in the Senate, they confirmed Judge Barret on that day in spite of the resistance by the Democrat Party. Justice Barrett was sworn in that night by Justice Clarence Thomas at the White House. She was formally sworn in by Chief Justice Roberts on the next day. In spite of the brutal grilling by Democrat senators during the hearings, Judge Amy Coney Barrett showed her qualifications as a jurist. She conducted herself with grace and exhibited her knowledge of the law and the Constitution. The only things left to the Democrat senators was to make the hearings a political statement on their positions on the Affordable Care Act and *Roe vs. Wade*.

It is important today more than ever to remind ourselves that in spite of all we are currently going through, the good and the bad, we must hold on to the thought that we have a lot to be thankful for. I thank God every day that I was blessed to be born in this great country. Nothing is ever perfect, but I am grateful for the important things—freedom from persecution, freedom of speech, the right to vote, freedom of religion, and our Second Amendment right to own and bear arms. It is worth holding on to these American traditions and cherishing them. Only then will every American feel secure and remain confident in our great country.

There is good news on the foreign policy front. The Abraham Accord is the peace agreements signed between Israel and the United Arab Emirates and the country of Bahrain. This is a landmark peace agreement that many have said for years couldn't be done. It establishes diplomatic relations between the countries, and they will establish embassies in each. Trade and tourist travel between the countries is a tremendous boost to peace in the Middle East. Sudan just joined, and other Arab nations are expected to follow suit.

The Trump administration has kept us out of war, and President Trump is keeping his promise to bring our servicemen and servicewomen home. His foreign policy during his term has been exceptional.

The media also isn't broadcasting that the caravans of thousands of illegal immigrants that were coming to this country illegally have stopped, and the border wall being built on the Southern Border is now close to four hundred miles. Promises made, promises kept.

Congratulations to President Trump for these extraordinary peace successes achieved during his first four-year term as president. I have to mention here that the media has not reported on any of this or given it the attention it deserves probably because it does not fit their narrative. They have not given any credit to this president for his accomplishments to date. They are not likely to do so this close to an election they hope will be won by the Democrat nominee, Joe Biden. This is not just my opinion; they are very transparent about this.

The campaign is heating up. President Trump is down in the polls although he was down in the polls in 2016 and managed to pull out a win. This election is different though in many ways. First, most of the country is sending out mail-in ballots to the citizens. The justification is the pandemic, according to the Democrats and the mainstream media. The president argues that this sets the stage for mass fraud. For example, discarded and destroyed ballots have been found in different parts of the country. A man who set fire to a ballot box in Boston was found and arrested. In Paterson, New Jersey, four people were arrested for collecting and destroying ballots.

I was born in Paterson. I don't want it to become famous for this, so I want to interject here a few facts about Paterson. Paterson was founded by Alexander Hamilton and has a rich history. It is the home of the Great Falls, which started the Industrial Revolution in the country. It was long known as "the Silk City" because of the great silk mills which produced silk for many years. It was a great place to grow up.

All citizens feel the same way about their hometowns, I believe. Americans are proud and rightly so. That's why it is so sad to see these things happen.

We have many reasons to be hopeful and many more reasons to be thankful. For example, world peace, prosperity, jobs, manufacturing coming back to America, lower taxes, low gasoline prices due to our energy independence, a return to traditional values and patriotism, school choice, prison reform, health reform, Operation Warp Speed working on a COVID-19 vaccine that shows promise to be ready by the end of 2020 or spring 2021, the border wall, lower drug prices, and so much more! I'm just saying we must keep the faith!

KEEPING THE FAITH

How good, how delightful it is for people to
live together in unity!
—Psalm 133:1

It has never been more important for us to keep the faith than today. Literally! I can honestly say that it had never even crossed my mind that religious freedom in America would be attacked, infringed upon, or in jeopardy. I was taken by surprise. I did not see it coming, and yet here we are. "Evil sometimes tells us what they want to do, but no one believes them; they are ignored. Don't dismiss their words" (author unknown).

When the COVID-19 pandemic overtook America, the Liberal Socialist Democrat political leaders got the opportunity they were waiting for. They now used the pandemic to prevent Christians, Jews, and Muslims from worshiping. Churches, synagogues, and mosques must be closed until further notice, they told us. It is for your own good, they said. They lied, but we were afraid, so we believed them. We believed them, until we saw them allow protesters to walk shoulder to shoulder, unprotected and unimpeded. We believed them, until we witnessed those same governors and mayors allow shoppers to go to retail stores and supermarkets, as long as they wore masks and observed social distancing. They said stores "were essential services." We were like sheep blindly following these power-hungry, agenda-driven leaders.

It took a while, but we woke up. More importantly, President Trump stepped up. He signed an order making religious services "essential." Talk about fighting fire with fire. He is a smart man! When you think about it, we are so lucky to have a president who looks out for the people first. Not being permitted to go to church or a religious service made us aware of how easy it is to take away our freedom. As the old saying goes, "You don't know what you have until you lose it."

Thankfully, there is evidence that faith in God is on the rise in our country. This is not a surprise, given what we are experiencing in our nation and in the world today. Each day holds more proof that we need God, our country needs God, and the world needs God. That is the resilience of the American spirit. Try to take something we cherish away from us, and we always come together and fight back.

Many believers—including the housebound, elderly, and patients with underlying health conditions—have been able to participate in "virtual" religious services.

I can tell you that this has been a godsend to me. My parish priest, Father Ed, and our music director, Ryan, began live-streaming daily masses on Monday, Wednesday, and Friday evenings at 7:30 p.m. The vigil mass on Saturday evening and Sunday mass at 10:30 a.m. are also live-streamed. Parishioners who want to physically attend mass can do so at 7:00 a.m., 9:00 a.m., and 12:00 p.m.

In June, the churches were opened to parishioners who wanted to physically attend mass during the week and on Sundays. There are strict protocols in place. For instance, certain pews are roped off to maintain social distancing. Sanitizing stations now replace holy water upon entry to the church, and the kneelers have been removed. In addition, ushers are no longer making the collections so as to minimize contact.

I was initially taken aback by these changes, but like so many things today, we will eventually get adjusted and adapt to them. We don't have a choice right now, and I also think that these changes will be in place for the foreseeable future.

Prayer has increased, even public prayer. I was surprised but happy to see commercials advertising Bible apps so people could read scriptures online. There is even an app to help people relax and go to sleep to soothing Bible stories. Amazing!

There is so much to pray about today—so much violence, illness, and so much evil in the world. So many things I believe only prayer can help. I don't know about you, but from what I can see, we need nothing short of a miracle today. Prayer adds to our lives in many important ways. Prayer unites us, gives us hope, and strengthens our faith. Obviously, we need faith in order to pray. Faith is our assurance that our prayers are heard and answered by a higher power. It's as simple as that.

So what is faith? According to *Webster's New Collegiate Dictionary*, faith is the "belief and trust in, and loyalty to God; belief in the traditional doctrines of a religion; a firm belief in something for which there is no proof, complete confidence; something that is believed with strong conviction." It is all the above for me, and I would also add that my faith is my belief that this earthly journey is but a brief moment in infinity, a human experience seeking spiritual growth, and the fruition of the divine promise of immortality. Simply put, our physical bodies will age and die, but our souls will live on forever. I can't tell you how much that belief comforts me. I believe that faith offers comfort when we are frightened, hope when we feel desperate, and strength when we are weak. Faith supports and reinforces our belief in the love of God and reaffirms our purpose in life. Having faith in an afterlife (heaven) takes away or at least lessens the fear of death. Remembering loved ones that have already passed can give us hope because our faith tells us that we will one day be together again.

As I am writing this, I am looking around my office and on my desk where I can see some favorite pictures of family and friends. Some of them—my parents for instance—are no longer with me, but these pictures are a reminder of their love and happy times. The pictures and their memory keep them close to me.

Faith in God, prayer, knowing the Bible and its teachings, and being of service are the ways we can achieve our spiritual goal. That goal is the spiritual growth of our soul. We all have a purpose and reason for being born into this life. Each of us is born with unique talents and gifts. Spiritual growth, character, and self-esteem are all enhanced when we use our talents and gifts for the benefit of others and for humanity.

I often reflect on my own purpose. I have questioned that many times in my life. These days, I spend a lot of time trying to assess my progress on this pilgrimage or earthly journey.

During difficult, stressful, or lonely times, I turn to one of my favorite Bible passages, Joshua 1:9: "Have I not commanded you? Be strong and of good courage; be not frightened, neither be thou dismayed; for the Lord your God is with you, wherever you go." There are so many comforting passages in the Bible, but I am always drawn to this one. The thought that God is with me wherever I am and whatever I am going through strengthens me.

Trials and challenges are part of life. None of us can escape that, but knowing God and having faith is the anchor that keeps me grounded. Turning to him in prayer and knowing that he is in control brings me peace.

I am noticing a possible silver lining to all that we are facing today. For one thing, I am seeing ads on television promoting prayer and scripture reading. People who have not paid much attention before are starting to turn their attention back to God. That is a good sign. After all, who better to turn to in desperate times than God? And these seem to be desperate times indeed.

There are also so many acts of kindness being done these days. I love the saying, "When the going gets tough, the tough get going!" It never seems to fail. Bad times bring out the best in people. Ever wonder why you instantly feel good when you do a favor or do any act of kindness toward another?

In Dr. Wayne Dyer's book, *The Power of Intention*, he relates wonderful stories of people helping others and their acts of kindness. In the book, he describes what happens physically to a human being when they give a helping hand or perform any act of kindness. When we do something good, it makes us feel good because our endorphins are raised, likewise to the person on the receiving end. Remarkably, a person that even witnesses an act of kindness also has their endorphins raised, so they feel good also.

According to *Merriam-Webster Dictionary*, endorphin is "a group of hormones secreted within the brain and nervous system, and having a number of physiologic functions. They are peptides which activate the body's opiate receptors, causing an analgesic effect." So there it is, the more good that we do, the better we feel. It's a win-win for all concerned!

I was taught in Sunday school at a young age that we are born into this world "to know God, to love God, and to serve Him so that we may live with Him forever in heaven" (*Catechism of the Catholic Church*). We are also taught that following his commandments and serving our fellow man is the best way to serve God. The Scripture tells us: "The King will answer, 'Truly I tell you, whatever you did for one of the least of these brothers or sisters of mine, you did for me'" (Mathew 25:40).

The 2020 COVID-19 pandemic has highlighted so many outstanding opportunities to be of service. The doctors, nurses, medics, aides, law enforcement officers, first responders, truckers, grocers, farmers, clergy, postal workers, supermarket cashiers, and all the people that are working to serve us are all gifts from God today. We are indebted to each of them.

On September 26, 2020, Franklin Graham led a prayer march from the Lincoln Memorial to the Capitol Building along the National Mall. Another event on the same day called the Return focuses on a return to prayer and a return to God before it is too late.

What a joy it is to see people praying together and practicing their faith in public! What a good example and hopeful image in the midst of all the turmoil in the country and the world today! Nothing gives us a sense of peace and hope like seeing people joining together in prayer regardless of what their religious affiliation.

The Trump administration began with an emphasis on the freedom to worship. The freedom to say "merry Christmas" again without censor. Once again, we enjoyed the observance of a National Day of Prayer, and it was like a breath of fresh air. I think that was a turning point, and I am grateful for that.

We will get through these tough times together—with prayer, the help of God, and, of course, keeping the faith!

Heavenly Father, today we pray for your guidance and wisdom. Help us to get through today and each day. Thank you for the days that are filled with the joys and trials that are unique to each of us. Bless our families, friends, and loved ones. Bless our military, first responders, law enforcement officers, and all who work to keep us safe and cared for.

Father, we ask that you defeat the dreaded COVID-19 virus that assails us. Restore peace in our cities and among our people, and bless our great country.

In Jesus's name, we pray. Amen.

FRIENDS, GUARDIAN ANGELS, AND OUR SPIRITUAL QUEST

> To my guardian angels, seen and unseen who have accompanied me on this journey. You are always there to guide me, comfort me, protect me, and teach me. I love you, and I will never forget you.
>
> To my unseen angels: I miss you. I know we will meet again.

During the course of our lives, we human beings come to realize we are on a quest. A quest for an answer to an age-old question "Why am I here?" What is the purpose of my life?

Knowing your purpose, faith in God and life after death are what gives us peace and hope. These are very important to our physical and emotional health.

We are accompanied on this journey by our brothers and sisters in humanity. Each of us have our own individual goals, aspirations, hopes, and dreams. At some point, we discover an awareness of our souls and the need for our own spiritual growth. That discovery can come at a young age or when we are older. I heard a pastor say during a recent sermon that it is never too late.

A story Wayne Dyer tells in his book *Power of Intention* made an impression on me and comes to mind now. It is about a man who lived his whole life according to what others expected of him rather than following his heart. On his deathbed while his wife was holding his hand, he looked at her and wondered if his whole life had been wasted, and he was dying with the music still within him. The message is "Don't die with the music within you."

Our quest for spiritual growth and enlightenment is a personal one. We are on a journey, and we don't know where this pilgrimage will take us. What we do know, however, is that no one can live our lives for us. We alone make the decisions and choices that define us and chart the course of our lives.

My awakening came when I was in my thirties. I was always a churchgoer, and I felt that going to church and saying my prayers was enough. As it turns out, I have learned that there is much more to it than that.

I was about thirty years old when I got divorced. I was heartbroken and devastated. I thought I would never get over it. Although it took years, I did get over it for the most part. Eventually, I began to date. On one such date, I was asked a question that changed my life. During our conversation over dinner, my date asked me if I was "spiritual." I thought that was a weird way to put it, but I was quick to answer that I was a good Christian and practiced my religion. By his reaction, I realized that he wasn't speaking of religion. He said that he believed that this life is about connecting to the spiritual rather than the material. He went on to say that he believed that the purpose of our journey in this life is to grow spiritually in order to get us to the next life. I replied that it was food for thought, and indeed, it was. After that, I did a lot of reading, soul-searching, and introspection, which led to my becoming aware of my spirituality. I have been on that quest for enlightenment ever since.

Once I became consciously aware of my soul, I felt closer to God. I began to see God in every facet of my life. I began to give him the credit, rather than myself, for all the big accomplishments as well as the small ones. I no longer say, "Oh, what a lucky break" or "What a coincidence that was." I no longer take credit by saying, "Wow, that was a great idea I had," as I patted myself on the back. Now I just say, "Thank you, Lord." Whether I found my misplaced keys or had a successful day at work or a promotion, I no longer take the credit.

I see God in all the events of each day, and that gives me a sense of security. I have an inner knowing and trust that he is always with me. As I look back on my life and my world view then, I recognize my naivete. I am light years away from the "younger me," and I no longer take anything for granted. As I look back, I can actually see each time my eyes were opened. For instance, I recognize divine intervention in the times when people showed up at the right time and made a difference in my life. I can now see how their influence changed my path on many different occasions. Some were strangers that just showed up out of nowhere and made an indelible impression on me, and then just as fast, they were gone, and others stayed in my life. The seemingly chance meetings became symbolic directional signals, guiding my path, pointing me in the right direction, and, in some cases, protecting me. They were my teachers, who taught me, calmed my fear of the unknown, inspired me, and gave me confidence. Each of them helped me to continue on my pilgrim journey, renewed and enlightened. I call them my "guardian angels."

One example is the lady I met on my way to church one Sunday. My parents didn't go to church, so I went by myself every week. My mom used to give me a quarter for the bus and a quarter for the collection. Sometimes I would walk to church rather than take the bus. This enabled me to spend the money on a hard roll and hot chocolate on the way home. It was about a two-mile walk all told, but the buttered roll and hot chocolate was a treat that was worth it to me.

On one chilly Sunday, I decided to take the bus. I remember sitting at that bus stop and feeling sad and alone. I was about ten or eleven years old at the time. I noticed a woman there who was also waiting for the bus. She started to speak to me and told me her name was Winnie. She asked me my name and asked where I was going. She said she was also going to mass and asked if I would mind if she kept me company. I told her I wouldn't mind, and we went to church together. I immediately liked her and was grateful for her kindness and company.

We met at the bus stop for some time after that, and then it seemed, all of a sudden, she wasn't there anymore. I never saw her again. I missed Winnie a lot, and I remember looking for her at that bus stop for a long time thereafter.

I've often reflected on why that meeting was so important to me. I'm not sure, but I know she filled a gap in my life at the time. I don't remember anything about her except that she was kind, kept me company going to church, and made me feel safe.

My mother gave me a lot of freedom at a young age. For instance, I went to dentist appointments alone. Today, that wouldn't be allowed. I also ran errands to buy things from the grocery store, including cigarettes—another thing that doesn't happen today. I was on my own a lot when I was young. It makes me believe I have a guardian angel. Maybe more than one.

There were many "Winnies" along the way now that I think about it. Another unexpected angel in my youth was my aunt Mary. I say "unexpected" because I never met my aunt Mary until I was twelve years old. A twist of fate put us together. My mom went into the hospital for a simple procedure and was only supposed to be there overnight. I remember my grandmother stayed with us while my dad was at the hospital with Mom. He came home the next afternoon and told me to get some things together because I was going to stay with my aunt Josephine for a few days. I asked him why I couldn't stay home with my brother and sister. He told me it would be too hard for my grandmother to take care of the three of us, and besides, she would need to sleep in my bed in the room I shared with my sister.

When I arrived at my aunt Josephine's, she told me to go sit in the living room with my uncle while she made a telephone call. When she got off the phone, she told me that her sister, Mary, was coming to get me. She blamed my uncle for my not being able to stay with her. I was hurt, and I was also frightened and confused.

When Aunt Mary got there, there was little introduction. She came into the room and said, "I am your aunt Mary. Get your things. We have to go now." She was abrupt and stern. I remember Aunt Jo asking her to stay for coffee, but she declined. Aunt Jo looked uncomfortable, and Aunt Mary looked angry. I looked scared.

We left, and when we got into the car, she introduced me to her husband, my uncle Ted.

That was the beginning of a summer that was a turning point in my life. It turns out that my mother developed a staph infection in the hospital that almost killed her. She remained in the hospital a long time and evidently had a long recovery at home. I thought about home a lot and, of course, worried about my mom. It was Aunt Mary who comforted me and told me my mother was going to be all right. She also explained why I had to stay with her for the summer.

My dad worked nights, so my grandmother was taking care of the house and my brother and sister. My grandmother was sleeping in my room, which was shared with my sister. I was the oldest, so it was easier for me to stay with my aunt.

As it turned out, it was a good summer. Aunt Mary had three sons who were hunters and owned property and a cabin in the Catskills. Aunt Mary and Uncle Ted would sometimes take a ride there on the weekend. I remember how beautiful it was. My aunt took me for a ride in the Jeep, and I saw a deer up close for the first time. On the way back home, we always stopped at the same restaurant and had fried chicken in the basket. I loved it and remember it as the best fried chicken ever. When we had venison on the holidays later that year, I put two and two together. I don't eat venison to this day.

It was Aunt Mary who arranged for me to go to a Catholic high school. She also got my grandfather to pay for it since my parents couldn't afford the tuition.

During that summer, we did everything together, and we became close. Aunt Mary was very religious, and we went to church on a regular basis. She had a large statue of the Blessed Mother at the end of the hallway; she would have me kneel there and pray every night before bedtime.

I found out that the reason I had not met her before was because she had been estranged from the family for years, except for her sister Josephine.

Meeting and living with Aunt Mary gave me a sense of independence. I had never been away from home before. I also liked having her undivided attention. Because of Aunt Mary, I developed a deeper faith and became more deeply rooted in my Catholic religion.

If Aunt Josephine had not made that phone call, I might have never met Aunt Mary, let alone live with her. I would never have had the opportunity to go to that Catholic high school. I am the person I am today in part because of her.

Along life's path, we meet many people. There are those fleeting encounters, and then there are those lasting friendships and relationships. I believe they are all important and all happen for a reason. I don't believe in chance meetings or coincidences. I believe that if we are vigilant and pay attention, we will recognize the significance of all those so-called chance meetings, the effect they have on us, and how they impact our lives.

I recall meeting two wonderful women who came into my and my children's lives at a very difficult time for us—Gloria and Evelyn Papa, lovingly known by us as the "Papa sisters."

My husband left me when my son was nine and my daughter ten years old. To make a long story short, we had to move from the home we lived in to a rented apartment. We had to give up our little French poodle, which broke our hearts, especially my son who was so attached to his little Napoleon.

Things were tough since my husband moved out of state, and with the exception of two payments, I never received child support. That wasn't the hardest part though. The thing that hurt most was watching my children cry and want their dad. They couldn't understand or come to terms with his being gone, and for years, he didn't look back.

Years later, when my daughter was getting married, she asked if her father could walk her down the aisle. I was surprised, but I told her it was okay with me. I never spoke ill of him and encouraged them to have a relationship with him. He did come to the wedding, and we walked her down the aisle together.

I had a second job in a beauty salon on the weekends. One Saturday morning, I came in about ten minutes late. I explained that I was late getting the children to my mom because the sitter didn't show up. The salon owner, my boss, told me in a loud voice that if I were to be late again, I would be fired. I was devastated and embarrassed in front of all the clients.

That was when I met the Papa sisters, and they came to my rescue. One of the clients called me over, and as I took the rollers out of her hair, she offered me a job. She told me I would never have to come back to that salon. She said I could work at her home doing her and her sister's hair as well as other clients she would get for me on Saturdays. She explained that I could make more money because doing three shampoo and sets would amount to what I made for a whole day working in the salon. Not to mention the permanent waves, haircuts, and hair coloring appointments. She also told me I could bring the children with me, which eliminated the need for a babysitter. I was thrilled!

When I arrived at her home the next Saturday, I was surprised to find her finished basement had a kitchen and a space set up as a little beauty salon, complete with sink, hair dryers, rollers, setting lotions, hair sprays, and everything I would need to work. It was perfect!

When it was lunchtime, Evelyn would be setting the table with lunch while her sister Gloria was under the hair dryer. Those were the days before blow-dryers.

It was always a wonderful lunch with cold cuts, Italian rolls, and salads they got from the Italian deli and bakery in the neighborhood. There were also cookies and coffee for dessert. My kids were ecstatic. So was I!

As time went on, the Papa sisters were my angels. They were so good to me and the kids. They worked in a book packaging company in town, and after they learned that I liked to read, they would bring me and my children an assortment of books. After a while, we had so many books that I needed a bookcase!

I came to learn that these sisters married brothers. They also lived in the same two-family house built by their parents. A great love story! I remained close to them for many years. They were so kind to us, and we came to love them as family. Ironically, their husbands owned a barbershop in a nearby town. Years later, my first grandson, Patrick, got his first haircut by Mr. Papa, Evelyn's husband, before he retired. What a small world, and how connected we all are!

I recently met a couple who, on meeting them, uplifted and inspired me. What made this extraordinary was the fact that I visited them to give an estimate on a decorative epoxy floor system for their garage floor. I was in the flooring business at the time. After some discussion, they invited me into the home so we could discuss the project further.

They recognized my last name and mentioned that they had met my son and daughter-in-law. They even showed me a picture of my son's family. Another connection. They then showed me pictures of their three sons. I commented on how handsome all three were. He shared that his son was killed in a motorcycle accident. And not long after that, they lost their second son. I was brokenhearted for them and began to cry. He said that their faith was strong and was what comforted them through their grief. He then shared a conversation he had with his son.

They were driving in the car and felt a need to ask his son about his faith. He said, "Son, I know you go to church with us when you come home, but do you love Jesus? Do you believe that he came into the world, was crucified, and died to redeem us of our sins?"

"Yes, Dad, I do."

He pressed him further. He asked, "But do you believe that he rose from the dead after three days?"

"Yes, Dad, I do."

Then his son asked him if he remembered taking him to a Christian summer camp when he was young. His dad replied that he did. His son said, "I never mentioned it, I guess, Dad. But at that camp, we were taught scriptures and the teachings of Jesus. It made an impact on me. That is when I was saved, Dad."

That conversation took place two weeks before his son's passing. Bill told me he treasures that memory as a gift from God, comforting him and assuring him of his son's presence in heaven.

I said that I sent my children to the same camp when they were young. What a coincidence? I don't think so. Every meeting happens for a reason. That business visit lasted over two hours. That meeting uplifted me and was the highlight of my day. I was spiritually inspired by that meeting and value my new friends.

Whether it is a brief meeting, a seemingly chance encounter, a relative, family member, friend, or coworker, looking back, we may recognize the lesson for us in those meetings and relationships.

Whether we benefit from those challenges or not depends on our identifying them and using them to our spiritual good. Sometimes they are the teachers and we the students, and other times, it's the other way around. At the end of the day, I believe everyone that crosses our path is part of the puzzle that completes our life.

I am not alone. In speaking with my closest friends and relatives, I often hear similar stories of the people who have inspired them and made a difference in their lives. Relationships are a strange phenomenon. We are born into families, some large, some small. For example, I am one of three children. One of my friends is one of eight children. The makeup of our families changes the dynamics. Each family unit is comprised of love, happiness, and unity. It also comes with its own unique challenges. Successful families work together for the good of all. Communication and sharing honest feelings are essential to this effort. In *Webster's New Collegiate Dictionary*, one of the definitions of family reads "a group of individuals living under one roof and usually under one head; Household."

Friends are another matter entirely. *Webster's New Collegiate Dictionary* defines friend as "one attached to another by affection and esteem." You can have a friend for a day or a lifetime. A friend may move away, leading you to drift apart, and it may be that you don't speak or communicate for years. Then one day, out of the blue, they show up again, and it was as if you were never separated at all.

I believe it is also possible to love a friend more than a relative. It is said that you don't choose your family, but you do choose your friends. Friendship is a sacred trust. Something to be valued; it is a special relationship. "I do not wish to treat friendships daintily, but with roughest courage. When they are real, they are not glass threads or frost-work, but the solidest thing we know" (Ralph Waldo Emerson).

It is true, important friendships are strong, solid, and resilient. Friends are not judgmental, yet they are honest with us, sometimes brutally so. While others may placate us, telling us what they think we want to hear, we can count on true friends to tell us the truth.

With true friends, we can be ourselves. They know how to listen and are there for us in the good and the bad times. We trust our best friends with our secrets, our aspirations, our successes, and our failures.

They cheer us on, calm our fears, and make sure we never feel alone. A true friend is certainly a cherished and important part of our lives.

One aspect of a good friendship is the commonality of our interests. When we have common interests, we are assured of spending quality time together. Enjoying each other's company is an important component of a good friendship.

I met one of my dearest friends, Marie, on my fortieth birthday. During our conversation, she told me that she was also born on 27, and we laughed about having that in common. Over the years, the number 27 has puzzled and fascinated us. We can't get away from that shared commonality. A few years after we met, her dad passed away, and it so happened that he died on the twenty-seventh day of the month. It dawned on me that my dad also died on 27, as did my grandfather who passed away on my birthday. My paternal grandmother died on October 27, and my maternal grandmother was born on October 27. Over the years, Marie and I have shared many coincidences involving the number 27. It could be a coat check number or where we parked the car in the mall parking lot.

But the most extraordinary thing happened many years ago. My church was sponsoring a trip to Italy. I always dreamed of visiting Italy, and so I signed up for the trip. When the time came, I paid for it in full. Marie is a travel agent, so I called her and told her about it. She said that she and her husband, Steve, were going to Italy also. I gave her the dates of the trip, and as it turned out, we were going to be on the same flight coming home on the same date, October 27.

Marie and I met for dinner that evening, and Marie tried to talk me out of going on the trip. She said she had already canceled her trip because she had a bad feeling about us traveling home on that flight. She said it seemed like too much of a coincidence.

She walked me to my car after dinner and tried hard to get me to cancel the trip as well. I was unconvinced. I paid for the trip and was really looking forward to it. I wasn't going to change my mind.

The next day, I received a telephone call from the rectory office. The secretary said she was sorry but the priest cancelled the trip to Italy because they changed the flight to a smoking flight. She said she would be returning our money. I couldn't believe my ears! I refused to cancel, but it got canceled anyway! I still can't get over it to this day. An unbelievable coincidence or divine intervention?

And what does the number 27 have to do with anything? We believe there is something to this, but so far, we haven't been able to figure it out. We will keep trying, but until then, we will continue to look forward to celebrating our birthdays each year on 27.

I met Marie's husband Steve many years ago when I started my business. He became the insurance agent for my business and still is. Steve has a great sense of humor and keeps us all laughing and entertained. He has been a great friend.

Another BFF (best friend forever) is my friend Maryann. We have a lot in common. One of our favorite outings is our jaunts to the casino. Win or lose, we have a great day out that usually ends with stopping for dinner before we go home. We are also great shopping buddies. Even if I don't need anything, I always manage to come home with something, usually a new pair of shoes. Her husband, Ernie, and her daughters have also been great friends, and as all my friends, I view them as part of my family.

My BFF Judy is a wonderful pal and has the knack of knowing when I am feeling low. She always lifts my spirits and can always make me smile. That is not surprising; Judy works as Jazzy the Clown. She loves working with children and enjoys her clowning. She has the perfect personality for the job. Whether it be children's parties, visiting patients in hospitals, or nursing homes, she is a blessing to many.

My Greek "sisters" Kiki and Georgia and I have been friends for many years.

Georgia passed away a few years ago. I always refer to Georgia as my spiritual guru. We would talk for hours on end about our faith, God, the afterlife, and all things spiritual. I learned a lot from Georgia and miss her.

Kiki and I carry on the tradition, and I treasure our friendship.

Kiki and Georgia owned a restaurant and bistro for many years until they retired. Soon after, Georgia became ill with cancer and "transferred," as she would always refer to death. The Bonfire was a favorite meeting place for years, frequented by politicians, musicians, and all who loved the ambiance, delicious food, and entertainment.

Kiki was the gracious and beautiful hostess who greeted all who came through the door. After the Bonfire closed, I sat down and wrote a quick poem I thought described it. It was indeed a special place to me and to all who visited the Bonfire Restaurant and Bistro.

Remembering the Bonfire

The Bonfire restaurant was the place to be,
To eat, drink and dance, and feel carefree.
Where friends could meet to have some fun,
The Bonfire welcomed everyone!
The best food, the best music, and the best wine,
The best place to visit to have a good time!
Kiki and Georgia greeted all with a smile,
And they always made sure that your meal was
worthwhile.
The Bonfire, as we knew it, is no longer there,
But the fun, food, and friendships,
Will always be dear.

I have been a Rotary member for thirty years and am a Rotary International alumna. My many Rotary friends have become like family—friends like Florence, Dale, Marian G., Florine, Art, Joe, Dan, John, Albert, and so many more. Even if you don't see your name here, you know who you are! I love you all!

Our Rotary Club serves our community, especially our youth and senior citizens. We touch many lives and meet and make new friends in the course of our service to the community and internationally through our disaster relief efforts, Gift of Life pediatric life-saving heart surgeries, PolioPlus which is eradicating polio on the planet, and health and hunger efforts.

My best friend, Nancy, passed away in 2002. I was heartbroken to lose her. Nancy was really a sister to me. We were inseparable, and Nancy helped me through the toughest time of my life, my divorce. We shared many good times, and she even taught me country dancing. I can still picture her in her cowboy hat and boots! She was not only beautiful; she was kind and a great cook! We shared many family Italian Sunday dinners together. She suffered for many months with pancreatic cancer. I was with her at her home practically nonstop the last few months of her life, and I was with her when she died. I was grief-stricken then and still miss her terribly now. I wrote a poem in her memory and will share it here.

Remembering Nancy

A refuge where my heart has hidden
From this melancholy life,
A refuge where my soul was bidden
To shield me from my fear and strife.

Like a ray of sunshine through the fog
Or the cozy warmth of a firelit log,
Your loving persona brightened every room.
Your hearty laugh dispelled the gloom.

Your warmth and grace and country style,
Your strength to go the extra mile,
You set the example of how to be brave,
And I'll not forget the love you gave,
Although it was too short a while.

I'd walk a thousand miles to see your smile,
To see your face just one more time,
To shop and bake and spend precious time,
To once more hear your voice sublime.

Oh, Nancy, I miss you all the time!

I have learned over the years that each friendship is special in its own way. Each of us has our own personalities, idiosyncrasies, and traits that are unique to us.

It is a wonderful thing when all of these components mesh and a true friendship develops.

That is what is so remarkable and makes them so valuable and worth cherishing.

Friendship

As life's journey unfolds, one thing is made clear:
The friendships we treasure grow even dearer.
They are solid and true, and we value their trust.
Making that known is simply a must.
We can always count on their love and support,
And as we grow older, we treasure them more.
Friends are chosen by our hearts and our soul.
To make ourselves worthy is always the goal.
Friends come in all shapes, colors, and sizes,
Which makes our choices of friends truly wise.
Our lives are the richer for those we call friend,
And we count on our friendships having no end.

Another part of my life that I find fulfilling and gratifying is my role as a religious education teacher. I began teaching when my children were very young and in a parochial school. I was absent at the meeting when everyone got to choose the grade they wanted to teach. No one chose the fifth grade, so I was elected. As it turned out, it was a great experience. As years went by, I taught the upper grades, which I enjoyed, especially the eighth grade.

At present, I teach sixth graders religious education. They ask questions that sometimes surprise me. For instance, some of the things they ask about are angels, death, heaven, our souls as well as the things that they fear and don't understand. They are exposed to so much on television. How can they not be afraid?

As far as death is concerned, I explain that our physical life starts with our birth, and even if we live to be 150 years old, our physical life does end, but the good news is that our souls live forever—meaning, we never die. They always looked relieved to hear that.

I tell them that what happens during our lifetime here is what is important. We each have a purpose and are put here on earth for a reason. Each of us is born with talents and gifts that are unique to us. It is up to us to use them to the good of all as well as achieving our goals.

I believe in teaching young children to be kind and to share with others, including their brothers or sisters. Sounds simple, doesn't it? But children are not born with a generous nature. It has to be taught. They have to be taught a reason to share. So I give them examples that I think they can relate to as well as examples of acts of kindness, such as helping a senior citizen neighbor carry their groceries. They always look surprised when I emphasize helping Mom with the dishes and other chores or helping siblings with their homework. As my dad used to say, "Charity and kindness begin at home."

I always feel gratified when I see the look of relief on their faces when I explain that we have nothing to fear as long as we put our trust in God. I am amazed at their interest in and their grasp of the Bible. Their brains are like sponges, absorbing scriptures and the lessons. I am always uplifted when I am on the way home and I reflect on the class and the lesson. Their respect and trust reinforce my commitment to teaching. It also gives me hope for their generation.

On occasion, I receive an unexpected handwritten thank-you note on a Christmas or Easter card. That note means more to me at the time than all my Christmas gifts. I am so thankful for the children in my class. I am grateful too for the opportunity to teach and hopefully have some impact on their young lives.

Unfortunately, the COVID-19 has interrupted our classes since schools are just reopening with adjusted schedules. So I am forced to take a hiatus. I am looking forward to an end to this upheaval of our lives and a return to some semblance of normalcy.

Young or old, everyone goes through trials. It is inescapable. We know that trials are inevitable and that we can all expect to face some adversity in this life. But still, we ask why. It seems to me that how we deal with each trial is key. In other words, it is not what we are dealt but how we deal with them that makes the difference. It may very well be that these trials can be used as lessons to be learned as we continue on our spiritual journey.

Some trials are trivial and some more challenging, but in this life, loss is the hardest blow of all. And grief is the hardest to bear. That is what makes faith so important because faith gives us hope. Hope and the belief that we are not in this alone.

Faith in God gives believers a sense of security and peace. I can't imagine my life without the belief that God is with me. How awful it would be to think that this physical life is all there is. Common sense and an inner knowing tell us something different. Sadly, too many have become numb to their inner spirit, their souls. I once read that each human being has that inner instinct, but some people deliberately ignore it. They become numb to their spirit. Some become so focused on the material that they don't recognize the spiritual or just don't want to. What a tragedy it would be to face the end of our lives and think that our lives had no meaning or purpose. I can't imagine that. I am so grateful for my faith and personal relationship with Jesus.

I recall something I heard a long time ago in an old *M*A*S*H* episode. Someone said, "There are no atheists in foxholes." I believe it's true. I believe we all instinctively turn to God in our darkest hour, and I have faith that God is always there regardless of any past rejection of him. It is never too late. Have faith. I'm afraid we are going to need it.

THE CHALLENGES WE FACE

The primary challenge today is defeating the COVID-19 pandemic that plagues our country and the world.

There is good news and bad news on this front. While it is true that most states are doing well, there are many states—including California, Florida, Texas, New York, New Jersey, and others—that are seeing an alarming rise in COVID-19 infections. That being said, the death rate, so far, is declining although the mainstream media and some scientists, including Dr. Fauci, are focusing on the worst-case scenario. I hope and pray they are proven wrong.

The highest death rate has been, and still is, among the elderly in nursing homes and assisted-living facilities as well as patients with underlying health conditions, such as diabetes, heart disease, auto-immune diseases, and obesity. To date, there have been 150 million plus COVID-19 tests in the United States, and the testing continues and is growing. There is a case to be made that the more tests that are conducted, the more positive cases are discovered. It is also true that more patients are recovering due to newer medications and therapeutic treatments, and many positive cases are asymptomatic. Vaccines are on the way, and new therapeutics are being used in hospitals to treat COVID-19 patients.

Our economy is another great challenge. In January 2020, our country saw the greatest economy in history. Unemployment for all demographics were at an all-time low. Manufacturing was thriving as companies were coming back to America due to the corporate tax cuts and reduction in regulations. Things were certainly looking good for America, and President Trump was on the way to an easy victory in November's presidential election. Then, without warning, the COVID-19 pandemic struck America and the world. Then due to the threat COVID-19 posed, President Trump shut down the economy he was so proud of, for the good of the people. Was this pandemic a coincidence? Maybe not.

On September 22, 2020, President Trump addressed the United Nations. It was virtual and one of his shorter speeches. However, it was a powerful rebuke of China and their handling of the COVID-19 outbreak in Wuhan, China. When the infections broke out, China stopped all travel from Wuhan to the rest of mainland China so as to limit infections. However, China did not restrict travel from China to the rest of the world. Consequently, a worldwide pandemic ensued. To date, there are 31,409,623 confirmed cases; 966,574 deaths; and 21,543,874 recovered cases in the world. The Chinese Communist Party hoarded personal protective equipment and, along with the World Health Organization, told the world that the virus was not transmitted human to human. The facts did not come out until the disease was spreading worldwide.

The first case of COVID-19 was diagnosed in the United States on January 21, 2020. On January 31, 2020, President Trump halted all travel to and from China. At that time, Joe Biden called him xenophobic and accused him of fearmongering. When they lie during campaigning, do they think the people have forgotten?

According to the BBC (British Broadcasting Corporation) on March 12, 2020, the president also suspended travel from Europe in an effort to stop the spread of the disease. This has potentially saved millions of lives we are told, although he was criticized by former vice president Joe Biden, his opponent in this election. According to the Dailywire.com, Biden tweeted, "A wall will not stop the virus and banning all travel from Europe or any other part of the world will not stop it. This disease could impact every nation and any person on the planet and we need a plan to combat it."

Congressman Dan Crenshaw (representative from Texas) fired back a tweet demolishing Biden's argument. Crenshaw wrote, "First, a wall will quite literally stop a virus. It's kind of the whole point of a quarantine for instance. Second, assuming you [Biden] meant this metaphorically, health experts, like Dr. Fauci and everyone else,

agreement. It seems she believes this will help their candidates win the November election. However, it looks like that tactic may backfire. Democrat voters also need the assistance she is blocking. Time will tell how when and if this second stimulus will reach the people who need it most, but as it stands now, it will not be before the election. The selfishness of the shortsighted Pelosi and the Democrats is mind-boggling.

Google, the tech giant, announced today that their workers will continue to work remotely from home rather than return to their offices. They will not return to the workplace until 2021.

Congress is still debating on how to hold China accountable. Meanwhile, 217,700 Americans have died while 7,979,885 confirmed cases have been infected as of October 16, 2020. Our economy was shut down. Businesses large and small were ordered closed as well as our churches and schools.

President Trump negotiated a new trade deal with China, and America was collecting billions of dollars from China from tariffs instead of China taking billions from us, as they have done for years. In the new trade agreement, China promised to buy grain from our farmers, but due to the escalating tensions, they have not done so until now. They recently made the largest purchase of corn from our farmers to date according to our president. We are also continuing to collect tariffs from China. However, things look like they will get worse before they get better.

There are evil forces working against our country today. Our great challenge is to defeat them. I marvel at President Trump's stamina and his determination to have our country succeed. Thank God, his efforts are nonstop, and his energy is amazing. I pray he is successful in defeating those who would work to defeat us. That is not limited to China. However, at the moment, China is the biggest threat to us and the world they envision conquering.

We have threats that are closer to home unfortunately. We are being challenged from within. It is frightening to see the deep state, the radical Socialist Democrats, and the RINOs (Republicans In Name Only) in Washington DC threaten our way of life. The mainstream media (fake news), Silicon Valley big tech companies, like Twitter and Facebook, are in lockstep with radical Socialist Democrats to influence the presidential election. They are also ignoring the civil unrest assailing some of our biggest cities across the country today.

There is mass lawlessness, looting, riots, and violence that are going unchallenged. The federal government is assisting, but it is an uphill battle because of the Democrat leadership in these states that are condoning this violence rather than ending it. They still are not permitting the police to do their job and restore order.

We are in a real fight for our freedom. Liberal Left political leaders have been attacking our freedom for many years. We just haven't paid attention. Until now. Whether it was taking prayer out of schools and public places, restricting our freedom of speech, or surreptitiously attacking our Second Amendment right, which is probably the most frightening. When the right to defend yourself is taken away, you are on a downward spiral toward Communism.

The Democrat nominee for president, former vice president Joe Biden, has already put Beto O'Rourke of Texas in charge of "getting our guns" if he is elected. O'Rourke advocated for this when he was running for president in 2016. His campaign promise was "I'm coming to get your guns!"

If we don't stop those who would tear up our Constitution and Declaration of Independence, who would erase our history and remake our country? We are surely lost. How could we trust people who do not love our beloved country and all that it stands for?

We are also faced with the challenge of educating our children in a free and peaceful environment, rather than in a restricted and controlled environment. Progressive Liberal professors and teachers are trying to control what our children are reading and learning. Students with opposite opinions are reluctant to express their own views for fear of rejection or failing grades.

I constantly ask myself how this is possible in our free country. For the sake of our children's education, we must advocate for school choice.

The Democrat Party and the strong teachers' unions want to eliminate charter schools altogether. They are also lobbying against private and parochial schools. If they are successful, it would force children from low-income families to go to inferior public schools in areas where it is proved that children are failing. The teachers' unions are lobbying to take away school choice and other options for children. If Democrats are elected, they promise this would become a reality.

Families should have the choice of where and how their children are educated to ensure their success. Other options that should continue to be available to them are virtual charter schools, minischools, prekindergarten, and other programs. We must also protect our parochial and private schools.

The school choice movement is in high gear, and I hope it will be successful. We owe it to our young people to get the best education possible.

The School Choice Now Act was introduced in July by Senator Lamar Alexander (representative from Tennessee), the committee chairman, and Senator Tim Scott (representative from South Carolina), a fellow committee member. The legislation would provide a "one-time" emergency federal funding for state-approved scholarship-granting organizations to provide families with "direct educational assistance." This assistance would help them pay for things, like private school tuition and homeschooling expenses. This emergency funding would constitute 10 percent of emergency education aid for state education departments and local school districts. The legislation was stonewalled by the Democrats.

On June 17, 2020, speaking to reporters while announcing an executive order on law enforcement reform, President Trump said, "We're fighting for school choice, which really is the civil rights issue of all time in this country." Frankly, school choice is the civil rights statement of the year, of the decade, and probably beyond. Because all children have to have access to quality education.

The Democrat politicians are also the ones arguing to keep schools closed in September.

Our children need to be safely back to school to ensure their education and also their mental health. Children need to exercise their social skills in order to be healthy. Our children are our treasure and represent our future. Their education and success are essential.

The baseball season opened, and teams were scheduled to play their first games, albeit without fans in the stadiums. However, the Miami Marlins cancelled their first game of the season due to four of the players testing positive for COVID-19. The very next day, the number of infections in the team was seventeen. The owners have put the season on hold for the Marlins.

Philadelphia was scheduled to play the Yankees, but due to several Philadelphia team members testing positive, that game was also canceled.

The good news is that the World Series was played, and the Rays lost to the Dodgers—2 to 4.

The 2020 pandemic was the excuse these Liberal leaders used to compel us to stay home for three months, separate us from our families, close our churches and synagogues, and close our schools and businesses. For a while, we were helpless to fight them. Or so we believed. After all, we all wanted to remain safe from the COVID-19 coronavirus, right? So we acquiesced.

Don't get me wrong; social distancing, wearing facial masks, frequent handwashing, and sanitizing save lives, protect us, and so must continue. Continuing the enhanced hygiene is not a bad idea, virus or not.

Originally, the models that said that two plus million Americans would die were obviously wrong. They weren't even close. That was not the only misinformation, however. Clearly, we were lied to. We know that because the advice and reports from the experts kept changing.

Remember when, in February 2020, Democrat Speaker Nancy Pelosi walked through Chinatown in San Francisco telling her constituents and the television viewers that there was nothing to worry about? "Come out to Chinatown and enjoy the restaurants," she said. She even had the nerve to criticize our president for banning travel from China to the United States on January 31, 2020. Turns out she was wrong and the president was right. Did that stop her? No. She then switched gears and said that President Trump didn't act early enough! I guess she forgot her February tour of Chinatown in San Francisco. Or maybe she thought we wouldn't notice.

The fact remains that President Trump's ban on travel from China on January 31, 2020, saved many thousands of American lives. Pelosi and Biden cannot change the facts, their lies, and criticism notwithstanding.

In many places and situations, we are being denied our right to life, liberty, and the pursuit of happiness—rights given to all Americans by our Constitution and Declaration of Independence. Our quality of life is being diminished by many evils afflicting us, such as the China virus, the terrible violence and crime, the riots and looting, the drug crisis, illegal immigration, drug and human trafficking, abortion, infanticide, lack of respect for authority, disrespect for our country's great American flag, and the seeming decline in patriotism. We are under siege, and we have the policies of the Democrat Party to thank for it. It is the Democrat-run states that are in the most trouble today. Just turn on the news, the honest news, if you can find it. When will people get tired of being lied to?

Unbelievably, some don't care about truth. They press on with the stubborn delusion that all is well in the Democrat Party. They don't want to admit the truth, wanting to keep the public in the dark, but the truth is coming out.

Parents today are facing a challenge as well. They are the first line of defense for their children. In the best of times, parenting is not easy. It takes love, patience, discipline, and a watchful eye. It also takes due diligence and time. Time is the commodity that is most scarce and is often limited because both parents work. It is even more difficult for single parents.

The truth of the matter is that the absence of Judeo-Christian values is responsible for the evil creeping into our television shows, movies, and violent video games. Parents are accustomed to making playdates for our children and arranging their social lives. The pandemic has put a halt on that, and a lot of parents are afraid to let their children go outdoors to play. So what now? Video games, iPhones, iPads, and computers have become the babysitters. They are keeping the kids occupied, inside, and safe. But how safe are they?

There is much debate about today's violent video games. To be fair, I understand that some parents are also playing these games.

The proponents of these games say that they increase dexterity and exercises their brains. They claim that these are only games and that they keep the children occupied. Others say these violent games desensitize the gamers to killing.

I happen to agree with the latter for what it's worth. While it is true that these are animated human figures, I believe it is a form of violence our children are exposed to that is unnecessary and dangerous.

In the end, it is the parents who will have to judge for themselves and make that call.

What happened to having a game of shooting hoops or old-fashioned outdoor activities, fresh air, and exercise? Less indoor and sedentary activities and more outdoor activities may also lead to decreasing childhood obesity—another benefit that should not be overlooked.

Parents want to keep their children safe and raise them in a peaceful environment with good moral values, but that isn't easy today, given what our children are being exposed to. Television shows and movies that are popular today expose today's youth to movies and shows that would not have been allowed to air in my generation. It is true that parents have control over this to a certain extent, but supposedly innocent or "family" shows easily escape such scrutiny. Unfortunately, we live in a hedonistic and materialistic culture today. We see the truth of that when we take a look at what is put out in the public arena today. Truth, honesty, and decency are often missing. There has been a moral decline in our society that is unmistakable.

Teaching our kids right from wrong and good moral values are the most important responsibility of a parent, but it is often an uphill battle today. What children are seeing on some of the shows on TV and in the movies as well as peer pressure make it more difficult, but I also know many parents that take their kids to see movies that are rated "parental guidance suggested" or "not recommended for children under 13" or even rated R for violence.

There are some good changes happening in the cinema in recent years though. There are more Christian-based movies written and produced by actor Roma Downey and others. Again, it is the parents' call. It is a matter of choice.

Let's not forget our children's iPhones and iPads. Children today are texting nonstop, not to mention that they have the Internet at their disposal. I see it in my own family. When my family comes to my home for a family dinner or get-together, I have to remind my grandchildren to put away the phones during dinner. Sometimes I have to smile, thinking about what my own father would say if he were alive today. He would tell them only once, and I know they wouldn't have to be reminded again.

Thankfully, there is a movement today to let God back into our schools. Some communities have allowed prayer back in their schools already, although this is not widely publicized by the media. That movement took on steam following the tragic rash of mass shootings in a number of schools in our country several years ago. For a while, it seemed like every time we turned on the news, we saw the panic, chaos, and mourning of another tragic school shooting. We watched as parents, teachers, and students automatically started praying; and we prayed along with them. They didn't stop to think about whether they were in a public school or not. That thought didn't even occur to them. They needed God then and there.

I've said many times that most people in their darkest hour turn to God and rightly so. Who else would you turn to? In times of sorrow, spouses, friends, and family offer love and comfort, which is so important. But only our faith in God can give us peace.

Today's teachers have a more difficult time than teachers in my day for several reasons. First, they are afraid today to discipline students for bad behavior. Second, parents and even the school administration don't back them up.

I am so saddened when I hear about the brazen disrespect for authority by some students. We hear stories of how some teachers are being abused by their students and, to make matters worse, are told by their superiors that there is little they can do about it.

Detention or going to the principal's office is often mocked, sneered at, and therefore ineffective. Ineffective because incredibly the parents don't have the teachers' or administrators' back. They side with the children, right or wrong.

I know if I got in trouble at school just once, there wasn't a second time because I knew I was going to be in more trouble at home. If I thought going to the principal's office was bad, it was nothing compared to the fear of facing my father after school. My parents didn't lay a hand on us. It was worse than that. It was the guilt they made us feel for disappointing them. Oh, and we did get grounded. I used the same strategy on my own children, and it worked. Hey, a little guilt never hurt anybody, right?

That reminds me of what it was like to raise my own children as a single mom. I know I wasn't a perfect parent, and that makes me sad. It was difficult being alone. I was always sorry about the things my children missed out on and all that they did without because of my divorce. They were so good though. They never asked for much, and they were very well-behaved. I always joked that God gave me good children because he knew I couldn't handle anything else. They were very young at the time of my divorce, but they were my rock, and we weathered those difficult times together. We became a strong family unit, and we still are.

Being a single mom who had to work, sometimes two jobs, was hard. But I remembered how I was raised, and I had that to fall back on when raising my children. For a while, we had to live with my parents, which made them close to my mom and dad, which helped a lot.

Up until the time my marriage ended, my children went to Catholic school. After their father left me, I could no longer afford the tuition. I was heartbroken when the principal told me that I either had to pay the back tuition or send them to public school. Ironically, at the time, I was working as a school secretary in the public school in our neighborhood.

When I went back to work after meeting with my children's principal, my boss noticed I had been crying. She called me into her office, and I told her what happened. She made me feel better by telling me that my children going to school where I worked would be the best of both worlds. That's what I did, and she was right. My children felt safe because they knew that I was close by, and I felt the same. God does work in mysterious ways.

Working in the school made it easy for me to work with my children's teachers and keep up with their progress. When parents and teachers work together as a team, children feel more secure and are better disciplined and better educated.

I was also a licensed hairdresser and worked weekends at my second job. I often had to take them with me to the salon when I was able to.

I come from a generation that prayed in school. We also pledged allegiance to our great American flag. Just those two things taught us respect for God, patriotism, love of country, and respect for authority. The values we were taught at home were reinforced at school. Those things are sadly lacking today.

This is evidenced by how our society has evolved. We are on the road to being a godless society, if the radical Socialist Democrats have their way. Which brings me to what I believe is one of our biggest challenges—instilling patriotism, love of God and country, respect for authority, and family values into our children and grandchildren. Many young people and millennials are spewing anti-American rhetoric and open distrust of our government. They are even suspicious of our great history.

Jesse Watters is a Fox News commentator who hosts the show *Watters' World*. He sometimes has a segment on his show where he goes to the streets to interview college students and young people in general. He asks them random questions about different aspects of American history, famous people, and events. I have heard him ask young people random questions, like "What war was fought in the year 1776?" or "Who was the president during the Civil War?" I am always amazed at the answers they gave; those young people had no clue. I found that so hard to believe, but when you look deeper, you learn that most students today are either just not being taught the history of the United States or they just don't care or both.

I just heard a report on the news today that a school district in Maryland wants to eliminate history from its curriculum! Unbelievable! Thankfully, President Trump's order to promote the teaching of history in our schools came just in time. How can young people appreciate the greatness of America when they are not being taught how our country was founded and the values it was founded upon? How can they appreciate how far our nation has come when they haven't been taught where we have come from? Unless they are taught our history, how can they know about the thousands of Americans, Black and White, who died fighting the Civil War that ended slavery, saved our great union, and kept our United States together? Or how patriots, of all races and color, fought in World War I, World War II, the Korean War, the Vietnam War, and the Gulf War and lived through the Great Depression of the twenties, women's suffrage, Prohibition, the civil rights movement of the sixties, and the attacks on 9/11?

Yes, America had and still has growing pains, not perfect, but always struggling, always continuing to aspire to higher levels. We are the greatest country in the world. We are admired by the rest of the world, and there are millions of people who want to come here to enjoy the freedoms we Americans enjoy and very often take for granted.

We are so blessed, but judging from current events, there are too many young people with anti-American ideas and misconceptions. Too many who don't know the history or greatness of our country, their country. Too many who do not respect our flag and all it stands for. Too many who are coddled and spoiled, so much so that they are taught to believe that they are entitled rather than being taught to work for what they want and earn their way. Being spoiled makes them weak; making them work makes them strong.

I have heard parents complain that some little league sports coaches have been told that there should be no winners. Each team is the winner regardless of the score. Where is the competitiveness? Where is the sportsmanship? How does that strengthen their character? It only makes them weak, in my opinion. I remember my father always taught us to be good winners as well as good losers. A lot of wisdom in that! Who is to blame? Parents? Teachers? Coaches? Clearly, we have failed some of our children, judging by current events, their lifestyle, and hearing their belief system or lack thereof.

That being said, there are a majority of kids today that do have a good work ethic, are patriotic and successful, and live a godly life. They are good examples for their peers, and that is a positive and hopeful sign. They are our hope for the future.

President Trump was the right man in the right place at the right time. I believe his election to the presidency was nothing short of divine intervention. He got our country back on track with a great economy, prison reform, police reform, controlling drug trafficking, and building a wall on our Southern Border and getting Mexico to help stem the tide of illegal immigration into our country. It is not publicized, but there are no more caravans of illegals streaming to our borders.

President Trump supports Christian values, freedom of speech and religion, and our Second Amendment right. His foreign policy has kept the peace and made us respected by the world once again. His economic policies, tax cuts, and deregulation gave us the strongest economy in our history. He has brought manufacturing back to the USA and fulfilled his promise of job growth. Under his watch, we witnessed the lowest unemployment rates for all demographics in history. Although the pandemic hurt us, the economy is bouncing back and our employment is also coming back, contrary to what you hear from Joe Biden.

Yet instead of defining the positive things he has done for the country in his first term, he is met with a hatred that is inexplicable. The only answer I can see is that he is standing in the way of those who would destroy our country.

Just today, I heard a well-known CNN pundit—I won't call him a journalist—say that if President Trump did his job and nominate a Supreme Court justice to replace Justice Ginsberg, then the mob should "burn the whole thing down." Mobs are descending on senators' homes and threatening them if they vote for the new nominee. This is despicable!

Thank God, President Trump did his job and fulfilled his obligation as president to fill that seat. And fill it he did. Justice Amy Coney Barrett is on the bench of the Supreme Court, which is now complete.

So we now face the challenge of a lifetime. We must fight to save our right to life, liberty, and the pursuit of happiness. This coming election is the opportunity to do just that. It is the most important election in our lifetime.

So how did we get to this state of affairs in America today? Looking at yesterday may give us some insight.

> Heavenly Father, our country is on a dangerous course today, with evildoers working to destroy us from within. Please guide us to a path that will lead us back to you and to your teachings. Bring our country back to good health, peace, and prosperity. Guide us back to the principles and moral values our country was founded upon and change the hearts of those that wish us evil. Please protect us and keep us safe. Amen.

LOOKING FORWARD

If you have a wounded heart,
Touch it as little as you would
An injured eye.
There are only two remedies
For the suffering of the soul:
Hope and Patience.

—Pythagoras

It seemed as though our country was living under a dark cloud for most of 2020. First, the COVID-19 coronavirus pandemic gripped us along with all the havoc it heaped on our country and the world. As if that weren't enough, we endured the protests, riots, looting, and burning of many of our big cities. This happened on the heels of the murder of George Floyd in Minneapolis, Minnesota.

It seemed that whenever the fog began to lift, fate or the radical anti-Trump factions, including Antifa and Black Lives Matter organizations, found another way to try to destroy our country and undermine law and order. Or could it be something even more sinister? Is it just a twist of fate or a coincidence?

I have to ask myself how that—right in the middle of the best economy in our country's history, lowest unemployment rates in history for all demographics, the highest stock market in history, historic trade deals, bringing our brave men and women home from Afghanistan and troops back from Germany, secure borders, school choice, prison reform, billions of dollars coming back to our country from China in the form of tariffs, manufacturing returning to our country, and four years of peace—all of a sudden we are afflicted by the Wuhan virus known as severe acute respiratory syndrome coronavirus 2 (SARS-CoV-2) and the worst riots we can remember. Keep in mind that all this afflicts us in a historic presidential election year. A coincidence? I think not.

Some people I speak with say that they wish we could fast-forward to January 1, 2021, and just leave 2020 in the past. While I understand their frustration, at my age, I can't afford nor do I want to lose any days I don't have to! What makes more sense is making every minute count to fight for our freedoms. I have faith and have to believe that America will survive and continue to thrive. Anything else is unthinkable.

I don't know, as I am writing this, how the election will turn out. Will President Trump get reelected? Will Biden and the radical Socialist Democrats win? Who will win the House and the Senate—Republicans or Democrats? The answers to those questions will dramatically and drastically affect our country going forward.

I am praying for the reelection of President Trump, but either way, I am trying to acclimate myself to either outcome. My father taught me at a young age to always prepare for the worst and have a plan. That way, I will feel that I am in a position of strength and control, instead of devastated and lost. Also, when I plan for the worst and the best happens, I feel that much better! That strategy has worked for me in the past, and it is a habit I have maintained throughout my life.

The good news is that President Trump has already altered our country's course for decades to come by his choices for conservative constitutional justices, such as Neil Gorsuch, Brett Kavanaugh, and Amy Coney Barrett for the Supreme Court who will uphold our Constitution and not legislate from the bench. He has also appointed three hundred or more judges to the federal courts—appointments Obama neglected to fill ironically.

Joe Biden, Kamala Harris, and the radical Socialist Democrats are talking about expanding the Supreme Court and adding justices to the bench. They are also planning, if they win the White House and the Senate, to add Puerto Rico and Washington DC as states. This will give them four more senators. Their plan would make our country a one-party rule. It will give the Democrat Party ultimate power and control by virtually eliminating the possibility of a Republican ever winning another election. Sounds like Communism to me.

We are already seeing the signs of our country going in that direction with the censorship of our news and restricted free speech and freedom to worship. Many freedoms have been taken away from all Americans in the name of COVID-19. Schools, businesses, and churches and places of worship are closed, on top of travel restrictions. There is talk now of banning families getting together for Thanksgiving and Christmas! Good luck with that!

Going forward, the Southern Border wall is continuing to be built, and our borders are secure. For the time being. Caravans of illegals traveling here to overwhelm our borders are a thing of the past. President Trump has gotten rid of the "catch and release" program that the prior administration put in place. It was a policy that mandated that illegals caught entering our country were immediately let go into our cities with their promise to show up in court. We know how that worked out.

Democrats say that if elected, they will vote to take down the wall and open the border. This will allow millions of people to flood our cities and our country. Who will pay the costs for those people? You got it, you will, not those politicians who live in their mansions and gated estates, like Nancy Pelosi, Joe Biden, Barack Hussein Obama, the Clintons, or Schumer. The poor and the middle class will be at their mercy, God forbid! Get the picture yet? It is a frightening thought.

What baffles me is that Democrat voters will suffer too. Don't they realize that? I have heard some say they don't care because they hate Donald Trump so much. Why? I don't know, but they do.

Foreign policy is another issue that is so important. At present time, America is at peace, in part because our adversaries know that President Trump doesn't give idle threats and means what he says, so they are afraid to push him. On the other hand, our adversaries are hoping for a Biden presidency for obvious reasons. They know his policies are friendly to China. They view him as compromised and weak. Worse than that, he seems to be in China's pocket, so to speak. There are ongoing FBI investigations that have recently come to light. More on that later.

All I can say is wake up, America, before it is too late! Our constitutional rights and liberties are being challenged, but they are safe right now. If the Left wins, they will continue to take those liberties away. The hope there lies in the conservative Republicans and the moderate Democrats who still have the common sense to rein in those radical politicians, Democrat and Republican.

On our side is our right to vote. If elections are kept honest—and that is a big *if*—we have a good chance of electing good, God-fearing people with integrity to govern us. I believe that there are more decent and levelheaded Americans than the anarchists that are trying so hard to destroy us. I pray I am right.

Either way you look at it, the winds of change are indeed upon us. Some things will stay with us for a long time. People will continue to wear face masks in stores and public places, and the social shaking of hands is going by the wayside for most. The frequent handwashing and sanitizing will continue as we remain cognizant of those around us and everything we come in contact with. Good hygiene is always a good thing and a good habit to maintain. Travelers and commuters are bringing disinfectant sprays and wipes to their hotels, subways, airplanes, buses, trains, cabs. and cruise ships.

The cost of the pandemic has escalated to a debt equal to the total cost of our economy. The current economic deficit is $25 trillion. There was a $1.9 trillion deficit increase for the first nine months of 2020, which is $1.2 trillion more than 2019. The Feds are digitally printing money to keep up by buying treasury bonds. Sooner or later, that debt will have to be faced. It remains to be seen how long that will take. In the meantime, our children and grand-children will have an unprecedented burden.

Another stimulus package is being negotiated by Secretary of the Treasury Steven Mnuchin and Speaker Nancy Pelosi this week. Pelosi is stalling. It seems she would rather have Americans suffer than give President Trump what she views as a win for him prior to the election. By the way, it is not emphasized enough that there are still billions of dollars from the last stimulus bill that hasn't been spent yet. I wonder why, and I also wonder where that money will wind up. This is another important issue that will be determined by who wins this election. Again, time will tell.

We are seeing our churches and religious institutions opening and having services once again, and we are thankful for that, even if it is on a limited and restricted basis. More and more people, including me, are tired of these restrictions and are going back to our churches and synagogues. I, for one, am looking forward to seeing a full church again.

Congress led by Nancy Pelosi is demanding that military bases be renamed due to the fact that they are named for Confederate generals. She is also demanding that all the statues of the southern Confederate generals be removed from the government buildings in Washington DC. It looks like she has won on that issue. These statues are another issue dividing our government and the country. Ironically, Nancy Pelosi's father, Thomas D'Alesandro Jr.—who was the mayor of Baltimore, Maryland, in 1948—had another view.

On May 2, 1948, three thousand looked on as then governor William Preston Lane Jr. and the late mayor D'Alesandro Jr. spoke at the dedication of a monument to honor Confederate generals Robert E. Lee and Thomas "Stonewall" Jackson.

As Mayor D'Alesandro accepted the memorial, he said:

> Today, with our nation beset by subversive groups and propaganda which seeks to destroy our national unity, we can look for inspiration to the lives of Lee and Jackson to remind us to be resolute and determined in preserving our sacred institutions. We must remain steadfast in our determination to preserve freedom not only for ourselves, but for the other liberty-loving nations who are striving to preserve their national unity as free nations.

Nancy Pelosi's father was on to something. His comments in 1948 seem to be eerily prophetic, as they could also describe the situation in our country today.

Incidentally, this was not widely reported on the mainstream media. I heard it on one of the conservative cable news stations and researched it. Americans are being censored and are not even aware of it. We must pray and work to keep our country free. Anarchists are at work to destroy us from within, a behind-the-scenes effort that has been simmering unseen for decades.

We Americans must not let that happen. I believe that we have been awakened just in time to save our country. I believe we will prevail if we remain united. We must tone down the rhetoric and listen to one another. More importantly, our political leaders need to listen to their constituents, especially the young generation. Our youth have the most to lose. They should be heard.

In spite of the cultural revolution happening in America today, I have faith in the American people and the American dream and ideals.

This is the greatest country in the world, and the good news is that if we stand strong and united, that will not change, but that is in doubt with this election. If we listen to the polls, President Trump is down and Biden is up. In a televised speech the other day, Joe Biden said he was running against "George." George who, he didn't say. Couple his gaffe of not knowing where he is or who he is running against, calling his ticket the Harris-Biden ticket, the major corruption scandal of his family unfolding, and Tony Bobulinski exposing his lies about not knowing about Hunter Biden's business interests in Russia, Ukraine, and China, how could he even have the audacity to run for president?

It is becoming clearer by the day that Kamala Harris, if elected, would be the president. Biden is compromised by his relationship with China and his corruption exposed. There is a call for a special council which looks to become a reality.

If President Trump is not named the winner of the election, it will be very suspect. The Democrats have done everything to control the outcome beginning with the universal mail-in ballots, censoring the news people can hear, and out-and-out blatant lies to the American people through the mainstream media. Again, people see this. I am trying to have confidence in their good common sense and love of country.

We have a lot to look forward to in spite of all that. We have the greatest minds in the world achieving great things in medicine, education, science, engineering, space exploration, and technology.

We are not as divided as the mainstream media and propagandists would have us believe. As long as we persevere in our beliefs and insist on the rights and freedoms provided us in our great Constitution, Declaration of Independence, and Bill of Rights, we have nothing to fear. One of those rights is the right to vote, and it is my hope that everyone in America will exercise that sacred right. It is, after all, a right, not a privilege. It is also our obligation as citizens to elect to office those that would govern us. It is more important today than ever. Sadly, though, it is a proven fact that in the past, many Americans, even though they have the right and obligation to vote, have decided to stay home. We can't afford to do that anymore. We must vote. We must be heard. Not voting is synonymous with staying silent. That silence will be deafening and the consequences severe. Our continued success, peace, and prosperity depend not only on the right outcome of the November 3, 2020, elections but all future elections. At the very least, we will have confidence in the knowledge that we did our part as American citizens to save our country.

We have many reasons to believe in a great future for our country. The American people are strong and determined. The "silent majority" is alive and well and are eager to vote in the November 3, 2020, election. The good news is that more young folks are going out to vote. One of the reasons is their desire to see an end to the lockdowns. If that is the case, they should be voting for President Trump since Biden and Harris vow a lockdown to stop the virus from spreading, which—I might add—doesn't have a prayer of working as is being proved out in Europe.

Going forward, law enforcement and police departments in our communities will be front and center news. We all know what having a decent and ready police force means to our communities.

I have faith that all eyes will be opened in time. Our future is at stake. After all, don't each of us—Democrat or Republican—benefit from safe communities and a free society? Don't we all benefit from a good economy? Don't we appreciate not living in fear of being locked up or canceled for our views or beliefs? In China, for example, people who talk against the Communist Party disappear. They are either being sent to concentration camps, prisons, or worse. Doesn't common sense tell us that the "free" Socialists speak of is not really "free" at all and may cost us more than we are willing to pay? It is beyond my understanding that these things have to even be considered in our great country.

July 4 is a day when Americans celebrate our Independence Day. It is a day when we remember our Founding Father's bravery in that steamy Philadelphia summer of 1776, when they unanimously adopted our Declaration of Independence. John Adams, who became the second president of the United States, told us to mark this day with "pomp and parade, with shows, games, sports, guns, bells, bonfires, and illuminations." We have been celebrating July 4 that way since 1777.

That was not the case on July 4, 2020. The day July 4, 2020, will go down in history as the first one without parades, fireworks, barbecues, and all the other festivities we have come to enjoy as we celebrate our freedom. Once again, the COVID-19 coronavirus is being blamed for the curtailed celebrations. While the threat of the spreading of this disease is a good reason for caution, I believe there may be more sinister motives at work here.

Too many freedoms have been taken away from us all at once in the name of COVID-19. Think about it, states like South Dakota, for example, led by their commonsensical Governor Kristi Noem, have not shut down and are doing well while states like California, New York, New Jersey, and others led by Democrat governors are experiencing a rise in COVID-19 cases in spite of continuing to be shut down.

I don't think I have to restate the obvious here. The radical Left wants to take away our freedom so that we will be controlled by the government. It is beyond me that people will continue to vote for them. I have even heard some Democrats say that they hate President Trump so much that they just don't care. I find it so hard to believe that intelligent, freedom-loving people really feel that way!

In spite of all this, due to the efforts of the army of volunteers that keep us going, life is slowly returning to some semblance of normalcy, at least in some places. People are tired of being shut in and locked down. It is human nature to want to be free. Look at Italy, for example. They are under a mandatory lockdown, and people are rioting in the streets in Milan and Rome. Where and when will this end?

Thanks to Operation Warp Speed headed by Vice President Mike Pence, a COVID-19 vaccine is on the way and the FDA has approved the use of the Gilead drug, remdesivir.

Regeneron is one of the therapeutics used to treat President Trump when he became infected with COVID-19. The president called it a "cure" because he felt better so quickly after taking it. He has authorized it for emergency use in hospitals throughout the country to patients for free. This is good news as the death rate in the United States is down substantially according to the news.

Americans are refusing to be held down indefinitely. Americans want to be free.

Note this excerpt from the Declaration of Independence, which is America's revolutionary "Charter of Freedom" and the document upon which this nation's founding principles were established:

> We hold these truths to be self-evident, that all men are created equal, that they are endowed by their Creator with certain unalienable Rights, which among these are Life, Liberty, and the pursuit of Happiness. That to secure these rights, Governments are instituted among Men, deriving their just powers from the consent of the governed. That whenever any Form of Government becomes destructive of these ends, it is the Right

of the people to alter or abolish it, and to insti-
tute new Government, laying its foundation on
such principles and organizing its powers in such
form, as to them shall seem most likely to effect
their Safety and Happiness.

These principles are what is at stake in the November 3, 2020,
election.

Last night—October 22, 2020—was the last and final debate
between the candidates: incumbent president Donald J. Trump and
former vice president Joe Biden. A lot has changed since the last
debate. As a matter of fact, there were several noticeable differences.
First, there was the calm and measured demeanor of President Trump
as compared to the chaotic first debate in which both candidates
excelled at interrupting each other. The debate commission shut down
the mic after the two minutes allowed each candidate to speak. That
probably helped. Second, the moderator, Kristen Welker, NBC News
journalist, by all accounts, including the presidents, did a good job.

This admittedly came as a surprise to the president and to his
base. Welker interrupted the president far more than Joe Biden, but
the president joked at a rally in Florida the next day that she only
interrupted Biden because he was running out of steam. Biden did
indeed visibly fade in the last thirty minutes, according to the critics.
He could be seen looking at his watch ten minutes before the debate
was to end. I think that speaks volumes. Many are comparing Biden
to the last presidential candidate who looked at his watch during a
debate. It is said that it is what contributed to George H. W. Bush
losing the election to Bill Clinton in 1992.

President Trump also pressed Joe Biden on the allegations of
corruption that recently made the headlines. A stunning October
surprise came with the breaking news reported by the *New York Post*
which reported that the FBI is in possession of a laptop belonging
to Hunter Biden. The *New York Post* reports that there allegedly are
many e-mails and text messages between Hunter Biden and his business partners implicating Hunter Biden, his uncle Jim Biden, and his
father, former vice president Joe Biden.

Tony Bobulinski held a press conference before the debate in which he affirms the validity of the e-mails and texts and the knowledge Joe Biden has of his son Hunter's "pay for influence" business dealings. Tony Bobulinski stated unequivocally that he was present when Joe Biden and Hunter discussed those business dealings. This contradicts Joe Biden's insistence that he never discussed his son Hunter Biden's business dealings in China, Russia, or Ukraine with Hunter even though Hunter traveled with his father Joe Biden to China, Russia, and Ukraine on Air Force Two on more than one occasion. Joe Biden was the vice president at the time and was put in charge of the US dealings with Ukraine, Russia, and China by then president Barack Hussein Obama. Bobulinski told Tucker Carlson in a televised interview that when he (Bobulinski) asked Jim Biden if he was concerned that this would hurt his brother Joe Biden should he run for office, Jim Biden laughed and replied "plausible deniability"—meaning, they would lie.

Around that same time, then vice president Joe Biden is seen in a videotaped interview boasting that he told Ukraine that they had six hours to fire the prosecutor or Biden would withhold $1 billion in aid. "Son of a ——, they fired the prosecutor," Biden said, so we gave them the billion.

It is reported by Tony Bobulinski's attorneys that he met with the FBI the day following the debate. He turned over all the documents, e-mails, and text messages as well as three cell phones.

It is also important to note that it has recently come to light that the FBI has been in possession of Hunter Biden's laptop since December 2019. There is reporting that suggests that they were—still are?—investigating alleged money laundering, tax evasion, and not registering as foreign agents. These are all felonies. These allegations are coming forth now—ten months later. Why has the FBI been silent? This would surely have scrapped the impeachment try by the Democrats.

The Senate Judiciary Committee and Intelligence Committee have been seeking documents from the FBI for a year. It seems the FBI has not been forthcoming even though President Trump has ordered all relative documents unclassified. I would say there will be some "'splainin' to do."

Senator Adam Schiff was at it again, saying that this was "Russian disinformation" and comes from the Kremlin. Of course, the intelligence agency shot him down and debunked those claims, but this man's lies are the gift that keeps on giving. He continues to embarrass himself. Enough already! You think he would learn his lesson. But the truth is he thinks that by just saying these things on television will be seen by viewers and believed by some. It's the old story of throwing spaghetti at the wall and seeing what sticks. So the big question is "Will anything come of it?" Will anyone be held accountable? I think we all know by now that if Biden is elected, this could all go away with a corrupt Justice Department under a Biden presidency.

On the other hand, President Trump would still be president until January 20, 2021. He has time.

The more that comes out, the more desperate the Democrats are to win the elections. I am praying that good triumphs over evil.

Unfortunately, one thing is startlingly clear—there is no doubt in anyone's mind at this juncture that there is a two-tiered justice system in this country. If you are a Democrat politician or a wealthy elitist with connections, the odds are you will not be held accountable. Just ask Hillary Clinton. On the other hand, if you are a conservative or a Republican, you will face the harsh scrutiny and full force of the Justice Department as well as being canceled and shamed by social media. Just ask Michael Flynn.

Case in point is the Michael Flynn case. Federal Judge Emmett Sullivan is still blocking the dismissal of charges against Flynn as ordered by the Justice Department and Attorney General Barr. Sullivan has now asked for depositions under oath from the Justice Department as to their reasons for the charges being dropped.

According to Flynn's attorney, Sydney Powell, the documents requested by Judge Sullivan are expected within days. They are finally reaching the end of the line. Sullivan is running out of excuses to continue his persecution of Michael Flynn, she states.

But, I digress, I want to get back to the debate. As far as the issues are concerned, both candidates put forth their views on health care, the economy, and the handling of the COVID-19 pandemic.

One stunning admission from Biden came when he stated that he would end fossil fuels and end oil and gas. President Trump countered with "I hope you are listening, Pennsylvania, Texas, Ohio, and Oklahoma!" Biden tried to alter his remarks the next day, but the Trump campaign came out with ads showing Biden stating his promises to end fracking and subsidies to the oil and gas industries in his own words. As a matter of fact, President Trump has been showing the videos of Biden in his own words on big screens at the Trump campaign rallies to get the word out—his way of informing the people because the media has not. Two networks that do are Fox News and One America News. Vice president candidate Kamala Harris is also shown on a tape from the primaries saying she is in favor of "ending fracking on day one."

One of my friends jokingly asked today, "Do they not know that there are cameras and audio all over the place today?" Indeed, it would behoove politicians, especially those running for office to remember that.

The Trump campaign raised $26 million the day after the debate and increased his poll numbers by only a couple of points. The Republican National Committee is challenging the polls as they did in 2016, but the Democratic National Committee insists that Biden remains in the lead. Again, time will tell.

President Trump is doing three, four, five rallies a day from now until Election Day. His energy is something to behold. It is hard to believe that just two weeks ago he came down with the COVID-19 China virus.

There is a stark difference between the two candidates. If Democrat Joe Biden is elected president, in his own words, "I will raise your taxes." He has also promised to shut down our states and economy once again "until the virus is gone." He claims we are in a "dark place, and it will be a dark winter." What a downer! We all heard in the debates how he plans to run this country. Contrast his and radical Left Kamala Harris's policy agenda with President

Trump's already-successful policies. He is the first and only president to bring peace to the Middle East! Think about it, the politicians all said it couldn't be done. But he did it!

I can remember during my lifetime constantly hearing about the wars in the Middle East and the attacks on Israel. We are not hearing that now. There is peace. That is priceless! Trump should get reelected on his foreign policy achievements alone, but nobody speaks about it. The mainstream media is silent on all his significant accomplishments.

For the most part, the mainstream media are an arm of the Democrat Party, and worse than that, they are censoring what Americans can know and hear about. Their agenda is to get the Left Democrats elected at any cost.

It is beyond my understanding. I keep asking myself, "Don't they have children and grandchildren they want to protect? Do they think their wealth will protect them? Do they think they are immune to the devastation of a controlled Socialist country? Are they that stupid?" They want to take our country on a bad path. Don't let them do it, America!

President Trump says that we are a country of "light," hope, and freedom and that he will, if reelected, continue his "America first" policy agenda. I don't know about you, but I much rather hear a message of light and hope than gloom and darkness. A country that is prosperous and free rather than Socialist and dependent on government.

Under President Trump, our Capitalist economy will continue as it has since the existence of our republic. He will rebuild our economy, which is already coming back strong. He will continue to secure our borders. The border wall is up to four hundred miles built so far and is expected to be completed by the end of the year. We will not be threatened with tax hikes, and our economy and our country will continue to prosper.

Another thing I am looking forward to is Christmas. We will be saying, "Merry Christmas and happy Hanukkah" again this year. Don't get me wrong; there is nothing wrong with saying "happy holidays." But the point is we can feel secure that we will not be "canceled" or shunned for saying, "Merry Christmas and happy Hanukkah" or for our beliefs.

I don't know what the future holds, but I think you know by now what I hope the outcome of this election will be. I am fervently praying for our country, the protection of our freedoms and quality of life, and the defeat of the COVID-19 coronavirus once and for all.

So here we are. It is Election Day. The polls are looking in favor of Joe Biden but have reportedly been moving toward the president, but polls have been wrong before.

President Trump did nine rallies between Friday, October 30, and Monday, November 2, a day before the election in a super push to the finish. Will it be enough? Are the scandals, the gaffe, and the poor forty-seven-year record of a tired-looking Joe Biden enough to push voters toward President Trump?

President Trump's voice is a little hoarse, but aside from that, he is as energetic as ever. I never saw anyone work harder than this man for his country and countrymen, not only in this campaign but for the four years of his presidency in spite of the obstacles thrown his way. I don't believe anyone else could have succeeded through all that adversity, including the COVID-19 pandemic. To his credit, he did indeed succeed in keeping his promises and then some.

I will once again, as I was in 2016, be up all night to the wee hours of the morning to see the results of the election, as I am sure will most Americans.

So who is the winner? If it is a landslide victory, we will know right away by the results of the Electoral College. If not, it may take days, maybe weeks or longer, to count all those mail-in ballots, not to mention the court battles that are sure to come.

America, be vigilant and on guard. Don't underestimate the dirty tricks of the Democrats though Speaker Nancy Pelosi is quoted as saying a few days ago, "The votes won't matter. Joe Biden will be the next president of the United States."

We are still trying to figure that one out. As Sean Hannity said, "If they tell you who they are and what they will do, believe them."

Buckle up, America! I know one thing for sure—it will be one hell of a fight! Stay tuned! May God bless the United States of America!

America

We are the home of the brave and the land of the free.
God gave these blessings to you and to me.
I will cherish my home; this is the land that I love.
I will always be thankful for these gifts from above.
God and country are close to my heart.
Please keep us together.
Don't tear us apart.

—Gloria Colli Counsellor

The End

ABOUT THE AUTHOR

Gloria Colli Counsellor is a proud mother of two and grandmother of seven.

She is a published poet with one of her poems "Autumn Joy" achieving recognition as a semifinalist in a poetry competition. Some of her poems can be found throughout this book.

She is also the author of *What Is Normal Now?* which is a book about the fallout of the COVID-19 coronavirus pandemic from her viewpoint as a senior citizen.

In addition to her passion for writing, Gloria enjoys traveling, cooking for friends and family, and doing volunteer work as a Rotarian.

CPSIA information can be obtained
at www.ICGtesting.com
Printed in the USA
BVHW081717160721
612126BV00005B/235

agree travel restrictions have vastly slowed the spread of the virus in the US."

Biden said he would have a plan. According to Vox.com, "Biden's plan takes a two-pronged approach to the coronavirus outbreak. First, he promises 'a decisive public health response' focused on free testing, improved access to treatment, the development of a vaccine and treatments, and increased healthcare capacity. Second, he calls for a 'decisive economic response'…" Of course, the fact is his plan mirrors what President Trump is already doing.

Many businesses, especially the smaller ones, closed, such as beauty and barbershops, nail salons, spas, gyms, restaurants and bars, small grocery stores, bodegas, and delicatessens, which were the hardest hit. Many have had to file for bankruptcy and stand to lose everything. New York City, the financial hub of the world and the home to many large corporations, remains closed to business.

The good news is that the American economy has a strong foundation and is coming back faster than anyone predicted.

Unemployment soared, with approximately fifty million Americans out of work and filing for unemployment benefits initially.

In order to aid the small businesses—those with less than five hundred employees—the federal government has put forth a stimulus plan in the CARES (Coronavirus Aid, Relief, and Economic Security) Act called the Paycheck Protection Program (PPP). The $659 billion funded under the Small Business Administration (SBA) is intended to provide loans to businesses to guarantee eight weeks of payroll and other costs to help those businesses remain viable and allow their workers to pay their bills. A $1,200 stimulus check will be sent to every American that filed an income tax return in 2019. A $600 stipend will be added to all unemployment benefit checks until July 31, 2020. Both houses of Congress are currently debating a second stimulus plan, and the outcome is uncertain since they cannot come to an agreement on the size of the plan or where the moneys should go.

President Trump and his administration are negotiating with Speaker Nancy Pelosi so that people will be helped sooner rather than later. Unfortunately, Pelosi is steadfast in not coming to any